CW01019654

Together We Thrive

Together We Thrive

*How to Find Your Tribe,
Build a Community and
Create the Dream Network*

RAPHAEL SOFOLUKE

PENGUIN LIFE

AN IMPRINT OF

PENGUIN BOOKS

PENGUIN LIFE

UK | USA | Canada | Ireland | Australia
India | New Zealand | South Africa

Penguin Life is part of the Penguin Random House
group of companies whose addresses can be found at
global.penguinrandomhouse.com.

First published 2024
001

Copyright © Raphael Sofoluke, 2024

The moral right of the author has been asserted

Set in 11.6/15.8pt Calluna
Typeset by Jouve (UK), Milton Keynes
Printed and bound in Great Britain by Clays Ltd, Elcograf S.p.A.

The authorized representative in the EEA is Penguin Random House
Ireland, Morrison Chambers, 32 Nassau Street, Dublin D02 YH68

A CIP catalogue record for this book is available from the British Library

ISBN: 978-0-241-70513-1

Penguin Random House is committed to a sustainable future
for our business, our readers and our planet. This book is made from
Forest Stewardship Council® certified paper.

www.greenpenguin.co.uk

To my wife, where my world begins, and the community takes shape. Together, we're a force. Your unwavering support is the cornerstone of my every endeavour, making you the most vital member of my community and my life.

To my parents, my first community, who planted the seeds of belonging and togetherness in my heart.

To my children, the next chapter in our community's legacy. May you carry forward the spirit of unity and strength.

To my siblings, with whom I navigated the landscapes of childhood, building the earliest foundations of community in our shared adventures and dreams.

To my friends, your support and laughter fuel my journey.

I love you all.

In loving memory of two remarkable men whose contributions laid the foundations for communities that continue to thrive and flourish. Their legacies are timeless, crafting spaces where people come together, grow and prosper, ensuring their impact endures for ever.

RIP Olu Oyerinde and RIP Bishop Karowei Dorgu

Contents

Introduction

Have you ever wondered how some people effortlessly establish strong personal brands and succeed in various aspects of life? What if I told you that the key isn't just their skills or talents, but also the communities they create and engage with?

Imagine having a supportive network of people who not only cheer you on but also collaborate with you, help you grow personally and professionally, and create a sense of belonging. This is the power of community, applicable not only to businesses but to all areas of life.

In my journey, I've seen how vital communities are for business and personal growth. I've faced tough challenges but also benefited from the incredible power of community support. It's this support that opens doors to countless opportunities, creating an environment where growth and personal development lead to endless flourishing.

'If you want to go fast, go alone. If you want to go far, go together.' This African proverb encapsulates the essence of individual speed versus collective endurance. Solitary endeavours might yield quick results, but the richness of experiences and true personal growth often stem from shared journeys.

The proverb emphasizes the importance of the emotional support, shared learning and diverse perspectives that community offers, strengthening personal resilience and creating an enriched life. In a professional context, it highlights the value of teamwork. While individual efforts may achieve immediate results, sustained success, innovation and significant accomplishments often arise from a cooperative environment.

I come from a Nigerian household of eight, with five siblings, and from the moment I entered this world, I was embraced by the comforting arms of my family, my initial and most intimate connection to the concept of community. Birth marks our inauguration into a web of relationships, where the tender bonds with parents, siblings and extended family form the scaffolding of our earliest interactions. In this microcosm, we learn the rhythms of communication, the warmth of support and the nuances of understanding others.

My family was my first collective, where I absorbed traditions, values and customs. It was within this nurturing cocoon that I took my initial steps to understanding, empathy, cooperation and the beauty of belonging. These foundational experiences of love, care and social integration were the cornerstones for my future relationships and interactions with the broader world.

I'm Raphael Sofoluke, a serial entrepreneur and the founder and CEO behind the UK Black Business Show, UK Black Business Week, Birmingham Black Business Show, Black Tech Achievement Awards in the UK and US, and Soar – the first bank-backed membership platform for

Black entrepreneurs in the UK. Back in 2017, I went to a huge business event, and felt left out because there was nobody else who looked like me. That feeling made me want to create a place where everyone, including people like me, could feel welcomed and included.

The importance of community within all my businesses cannot be overstated. My events and platforms bring together a network of individuals who share common goals, experiences and challenges, providing a supportive environment crucial for the success and development of Black entrepreneurs and professionals. We foster knowledge-sharing, mentorship and empowerment, while engaging and allowing allies and huge corporate companies the opportunity to connect with the Black community.

In this book, we'll explore how community-building can benefit your brand profile, advance your career, aid in self-development and enrich your social life. Whether it's in the workplace, where a strong community can boost your progress; in your business, where it can be the foundation for building your empire; or in your personal life, where nurturing meaningful relationships can lead to profound growth – together, we'll cover it all.

My experience of community-building has been an enriching experience, and I can't wait to share with you all the golden tips that I've learned on my journey. So, if you're ready to unlock the full potential of finding your tribe, I invite you to dive into the pages ahead and embrace the power of building a thriving community. This is the ultimate tool, and I'm giving it to you – because together we thrive.

CHAPTER I

Ties That Shape Our Lives: What is Community?

Have you ever felt that invisible tug, the unspoken connection that makes you feel part of something larger? In this chapter, I want to explore what community means and how it comes about – the magic behind these invisible ties that shape our lives.

It's important to understand exactly how our shared experiences – those quiet nods of understanding and moments of compassion – are the very essence of community. The connections we make with each other define our identities, influence our decisions, and ultimately form the backbone of thriving societies. Learning how the close-knit bonds we have with our friends and family have a profound impact on all our relationships, inside and outside of work, is vital for anyone seeking to understand the foundation of community.

In 2004, Dan Buettner – an explorer, National Geographic Fellow, and journalist – travelled the world with a team of scientists and demographers in order to find areas populated by people who not only lived a long time but also enjoyed a high quality of life in their old age. They dubbed these regions 'Blue Zones'.[1] The team discovered that strong social networks, a sense of belonging, and close-knit relationships – as well as shared lifestyle habits – were crucial factors when it came to longevity. The significance of community within the context of Blue Zones, where people live longer and have healthier lives, indicates the role of social connections in overall well-being.

Thousands of years prior to this, the ancient Greek philosopher Aristotle emphasized the importance of community in his ethical and political teachings. He believed that human beings are inherently social creatures, and an individual's fulfilment and flourishing are intrinsically tied to their relationships within a larger network of people. The concept of the *polis* (city-state) was fundamental to his philosophy, and he envisioned a community as a cohesive unit comprising individuals striving for a common good. Aristotle believed that the well-being of the individual is intricately linked to the well-being of the community, and he advocated for a balanced and harmonious coexistence where each member contributes to the greater good.

According to Aristotle, the cultivation of virtuous and ethical behaviour within a network is what leads to a just and prosperous society, encouraging cooperation, fairness, and the development of a collective moral character essential for the stability and advancement of everyone as a whole.[2]

I spoke with Andy Ayim MBE, a serial entrepreneur and long-term investor in entrepreneurs with global ambitions to change society and the world positively – in exactly the way Aristotle envisioned. He runs the Angel Investing School, a global critical thinking course for business leaders interested in investing in start-ups. In 2021, Andy received the prestigious Queen's Honours MBE medal for his substantial contributions to diversity and technology in the UK.

Andy grew up in Tottenham, North London, one of the most multicultural places in Europe – where more than ninety nationalities exist, and 300 languages are spoken. In and out of school he had friends from Pakistan, Scotland, Jamaica and Turkey, and from a young age he could appreciate the wisdom of the African proverb 'It takes a village to raise a child'.

When asked about what community means to him and how this has been shaped by his personal experiences, he said he could sum up its meaning with 'the South African philosophy of Ubuntu, which translates as "I am because we are"'.

'You learn to appreciate all the small ways we come together regardless of our race or background,' he told me. 'Small things like my neighbours taking me to school or playing football locally with friends, or eating meals and opening up a door to a new and exciting culture. As I've grown older and travelled the world, you realize that community isn't limited by boundaries and lines, as there is more that we have in common as humanity than what separates us.'

Ubuntu offers a powerful and expansive view that transcends traditional boundaries of geography, race and culture. With its core idea of 'I am because we are', it emphasizes interconnectedness and mutual responsibility among individuals. It suggests that a person's identity and existence are deeply tied to those around them.

Andy's personal experience illustrates how everyday acts of kindness and connection form the fabric of community, sometimes more than traditional markers of identity. These experiences serve not only as examples of Ubuntu in action but also as reminders of the simple yet powerful ways in which our lives are interwoven with those of the people around us. Community is often built on the foundation of small, everyday interactions, which together contribute to a sense of inclusion and shared humanity.

Despite the apparent differences that might seem to divide us, there are fundamental human experiences that unite us. Andy's realization that there is 'more that we have in common as humanity than what separates us' is a powerful message. It challenges us to look beyond superficial divisions and recognize the universal threads of human experience and empathy that bind us together.

This view of community, informed by Ubuntu, is a philosophical and practical guide for living. It calls for an appreciation of our mutual dependence, encouraging real-life actions that support and uplift an understanding of others. It's a reminder that our well-being is inextricably linked to the well-being of those we have relationships with and are connected to, near and far.

Like Andy, Izzy Obeng grew up in North London, and she shared with me how coming of age in her local area shaped her life. Izzy is an entrepreneur, business consultant and the founder and CEO of Foundervine. She also sits on the board as a non-executive director for Capital Enterprise. At Foundervine, Izzy leads a consultancy that aims to create systemic change in entrepreneurship. They support early stage companies, providing entrepreneurs from underrepresented groups with mentorship, training and access to capital.

'I grew up in a community that was one of the most multicultural populations in all of the UK but also one of the poorest,' Izzy shared with me. 'I found myself immersed in local politics as a young person, sitting on my borough's Youth Council, as well as taking part in protests against knife crime, and the kind of community disillusionment that would later see Tottenham emerge as the epicentre of the 2011 London riots.

'These experiences were transformative. They shaped me immeasurably, opening up my mind to unconventional ideas about ways to solve social problems, and frustration at a system that works for the few and not the many. They laid the foundation for the innovative ethos that would later define Foundervine. A desire for justice, for changing the narrative regarding who gets to become a business owner and who doesn't, played a vital role in shaping my approach to entrepreneurship, business growth and investment.'

Izzy's involvement in local politics and activism was not merely extracurricular activities, but vital experiences that embedded in her a deep sense of social responsibility and a desire for systemic change. Her experiences, far from being disheartening, were transformative, inspiring an innovative ethos that would later be instrumental in the creation of Foundervine. This initiative was not born in isolation but was the result of years of immersion in a community.

Izzy's drive for justice and her commitment to altering the narrative around entrepreneurship – specifically, who has the opportunity to own a business and who doesn't – reflects a vision influenced by her early experiences within a vibrant yet challenged community. Her journey from being a Youth Council member and activist to a pioneering entrepreneur exemplifies how community experiences can significantly shape your approach to business, investment and growth.

Someone else who has been active in creating a future that rectifies historical wrongs is Jamelia Donaldson. Founder and CEO of TreasureTress, Europe's largest subscription service dedicated to curly-hair product discovery, Jamelia has transformed the natural-hair care landscape. TreasureTress not only addresses the lack of quality products for curly hair in the UK, but also nurtures a vibrant community that transcends geographical boundaries. And Jamelia's influence extends far beyond TreasureTress. Recognizing the beauty industry's disregard for Black and Multi-Ethnic consumers, she has started up a consultancy arm within her company, empowering brands worldwide to establish authentic connections and find their rightful place within this underserved market.

Jamelia was able to offer insight into how she views community based on her personal experiences. 'Shaped by my experiences as the founder of TreasureTress and having built a "community-first" brand, I perceive community-building as a deliberate yet organic journey. Since the beginning of time, women in particular have consistently formed communities as a means of survival and support. Whether within familial structures, tribal societies or modern urban settings, women have demonstrated a natural inclination to connect, share and collaborate.

'TreasureTress, through its network, space and community, successfully builds, maintains, celebrates and increases the visibility of the experiences of Black and Multi-Ethnic women (and girls) and their hair. Through our prominent service for discovering products tailored to textured hair, I witnessed the impact of uniting people around a shared commitment to natural-hair care, a common passion that acted as a catalyst, forging connections that transcended the digital realm.'

Jamelia describes community-building as both a strategic and organic process, and acknowledges the historical context in which women have sought to connect with other women. TreasureTress has leveraged these natural inclinations towards connection and sharing in order to build a supportive network centred around the unique experiences of Black and Multi-Ethnic women and their hair care journeys.

Jamelia has created a space that not only serves these women but also celebrates and amplifies the visibility of their experiences. By focusing on the specific needs of the natural-hair care niche, TreasureTress has managed to forge a powerful community around a shared passion, illustrating how common interests can create meaningful connections that extend beyond the digital space. Her approach to community-building demonstrates the power of aligning brand values with community needs.

Moving from thinking about community on a macro level to a more intimate perspective, I spoke to Elizabeth Uviebinené, a multi-talented entrepreneur whose outlook on community invites a broader, more inclusive understanding of the concept, and values the depth and quality of connections over quantity.

Elizabeth is the founder of Storia, a journaling app that bridges the gap between individual introspection and the human need for community. Storia is a tool to organize your thoughts into themed journals, and discover journals created by friends or like-minded individuals. She is also the multi-award-winning author of five books, including the bestseller *Slay In Your Lane: The Black Girl Bible* (co-authored with Yomi Adegoke), which created a new category in the publishing market.

She has been named an Ad Age Leading Woman in Europe and a Marie Claire Future Shaper, and won a Groucho Maverick award for being a culturally progressive innovator. Despite being so recognized, when asked about how community has significantly impacted her life or career, she said: 'I have a community with my best friend. Contrary to popular belief, you can be in a community of two. Our connection was established during our university years, a formative period. University is where one typically finds their initial, crucial friendships, and ours unknowingly became a cornerstone for future careers. Being part of this community, especially away from home for the first time, proved exceptionally impactful. Without the support, I doubt I would have embarked on the journey to become an author, and my current career trajectory might have taken a vastly different path. The shared experiences, aspirations and values we cultivated together have broadened my horizons, enabling me to evolve into who I am today.'

This intimate and reflective perspective acknowledges the significance of deep personal connections that can indeed form a community, even one as small as two people. Elizabeth challenges the conventional notion that communities must be large or broadly defined by local or cultural boundaries. She emphasizes the strength and impact of meaningful, one-on-one relationships.

For Elizabeth, her university years were a critical period of personal growth and discovery. The fact that a connection she made then became a cornerstone for her future career speaks to the influence that such relationships can have on your life direction and choices. Her experience is a testament to how a community, no matter its size, can provide a supportive and enriching environment.

Elizabeth's insights also touch on the power of having a support network in decisive moments, such as moving away from home for the first time. The support from her community of two provided Elizabeth with the confidence and encouragement necessary to pursue a challenging and uncertain path. Her narrative challenges us to reconsider our understanding of community, and to recognize the deep impact that a single significant relationship can have on our lives.

Lynsey Campbell's perspective, like Elizabeth's, intriguingly challenges traditional views of community. Lynsey is a successful technology executive who has led many teams in some of the world's largest organizations.

Mum to twin girls, she is committed to becoming a leader who inspires others to connect to their purpose and operate with passion and integrity. Lynsey serves as a trustee and ambassador for a diverse variety of charities, with the sole purpose of improving the lives and career experiences of underrepresented groups.

'I have been part of groups officially labelled a "community" but the activity and support is not there, whereas I've also been part of informal groups where the community aspect is 100 per cent . . . Community is like a group "sense" and feeling versus an official brand or term, in my opinion.'

Lynsey understands true community is characterized not by a name or structure but by the quality of connections and the collective feeling it engenders among its members. The essence of community is something deeply felt and experienced on a personal level, transcending the superficial layers of designation or branding.

So, when we look at community and the importance it has on our lives, it's fair to say that it could be the difference between a good life and a great life – and the impact of community goes far beyond enriching the life of one individual. When we get down to the root of what community is, for me it boils down to shared experiences. Our communities are platforms for individuals to express their beliefs, values and aspirations collectively.

Whether we like to think it or not, we are all part of a community – either by choice or external factors. As the world continues to grow, we are developing new types of community in new and interesting ways. Our ability to connect on a global scale through media and the internet has allowed us to form our own identities and belong to a multitude of groups.

Now, let's take a closer look at some of the communities that we as people generally find ourselves a part of – or ones we could look to be a part of.

Types of Communities

Community of Place

This includes urban and suburban communities and neighbourhoods; rural, national and global locations; your workplace and your home. You are bound to a community of place because of where you reside, work, visit or spend a significant portion of your time. Because of this, it's important that you try to create genuine friendships in these places.

Communities of Interest

These are subcultures that are formed around shared beliefs and interests that can be distinct from the beliefs and interests of the dominant culture in which you live or work. For example, although my brothers and I are part of one big family, we all support different football teams! Being a member of the Liverpool FC community for me is a privilege, while my brothers have decided to support other teams like Manchester United, Aston Villa and Chelsea. When they meet someone who supports their team, they have a connection with that person, whereas even I as a close family member cannot connect with them on that level. Have you ever met someone and found out that they shared the same interest as you? Whatever that interest is, can you remember how you felt? It's a feeling of excitement, and there's an almost instant connection.

Communities of Needs

These are formed on the basis of shared experiences and needs. Members of these communities bond over their shared needs, and support and advocate for one another. Examples of these groups are disabled communities and elderly communities.

Communities of Practice

These include professional networks of people who share a career or expertise, guilds and associations, business groups and more.

Identity-Based Communities

These are built on shared identities and include religious and ethnic groups. People with shared ethnicity have a common history, practices, culture and beliefs. This leads them to come together naturally to engage over those cultural practices or beliefs. When you meet someone and find out that they too are Scottish, Nigerian or Irish, you instantly feel connected because you have a shared history or background that you can both relate to, and this makes it easier for you to find common ground.

Opeyemi Sofoluke is my wife and best friend, and we've built our own unique little world at home. Our lively household is made up of me, Opeyemi, our eldest son Reuel, our daughter Lolade and our youngest son Joshua. Together, Opeyemi and I have orchestrated some truly remarkable feats, and the prospect of what lies ahead fills me with anticipation.

When asked about identity-based communities, Opeyemi shared her experiences of growing up in the church, and how this shaped her own understanding of community.

'I find that the times in my life where I didn't feel part of a community have given me a real understanding and appreciation of what it means to belong to a community. An early memory that has shaped this definition goes back to my childhood. Growing up we attended a majority-white evangelical church in Rotherhithe. The church was nice and people were friendly, but even as a child I remember experiencing moments where I didn't feel like I truly belonged. My parents were committed members and had church-related responsibilities, I was part of the Girls' Brigade and attended Sunday School – as a family we were involved and active, but I just remember a feeling that is difficult to articulate, but I didn't always feel at home.

'Every first and third Sunday of the month, after church we would go home, have Sunday lunch and then head out to a gathering called the Overseas Fellowship of Nigerian Christians (OFNC), a non-denominational Christian organization of Nigerians that was started in the 1960s by Nigerians who came to study in the UK. The meetings took place in Kennington from 3 p.m. to 6 p.m., and I loved going. OFNC felt like another church gathering but it was fun, it was lively and vibrant – a contrast to my normal church service. All the adults were my aunties and uncles – they weren't family, but they could have been, and across the community there was so much support. Whether it was all the aunties offering to cook a dish for an upcoming birthday party, or the parents helping each other with childcare as many of our parents were studying at the time, OFNC provided a real community and I felt it as a child. There was a real sense of belonging.'

Opeyemi's words shed light on the impact identity-based communities can have on an individual's identity, and the subtle yet significant ways in which cultural dissonance can affect your experience within a community. Despite her and her family's active involvement in their church, there was a feeling that they never fully belonged.

The OFNC gatherings, characterized by the lively, vibrant atmosphere and familial warmth, offered a starkly different experience. This environment, in which cultural traditions and mutual support were prevalent, created a strong sense of shared identity. The use of terms like 'aunty' and 'uncle' to describe non-biological relations signifies the depth of the connections formed, reflecting a common cultural practice extending the notion of family beyond blood ties.

Identity-based communities play a critical role in providing a space where individuals can fully express and celebrate their cultural heritage. They offer essential emo-tional and practical support, enhancing members' well-being and sense of self.

Opeyemi's insights highlight the nuanced difference between being a part of a community and feeling at home within it, and the importance of cultural representation and acknowledgement within communal spaces in order to develop genuine connections. Identity-based commu-nities like the OFNC are vital spaces for individuals navi-gating multicultural landscapes, offering a sanctuary where cultural identities are not just recognized but celebrated, and thus playing a crucial role in shaping a person's sense of belonging.

Benefits of Community

The impact of community on individual well-being and health is a revelation that goes far beyond a causal connec-tion; it's an essential facet of our overall health and quality of life. Research has found that strong social connections help to improve mental health, reduce stress and increase longevity.

Health, Well-Being and Resilience

Blue Zones are a great example of how social connections are key to health and well-being. These communities in areas such as Sardinia, Italy and Japan feature astonishing levels of longevity and well-being among their inhabitants, and demonstrate the significance of close-knit social connections and mutual support.

The work of neuroscientists has shown that there are physiological benefits to human connection. Social interactions stimulate the release of oxytocin – the 'love hormone', which in turn inspires trust, reduces stress and induces a sense of well-being. The impact of oxytocin goes far beyond our emotions, extending to our physical health – potentially lowering our blood pressure, reducing inflammation and even promoting faster wound healing. Here we see the tangible and vital role of community in shaping our bodies and minds.

These relational links also offer a buffer against the hardships and stressors of life. Shared experiences and mutual understanding and assistance play a key role in helping us to navigate life's many challenges. Whether it's embracing the comfort of a social network during times of grief, experiencing the jubilation of a shared accomplishment or enjoying simple daily interactions, the emotional nourishment we derive from community acts as a shield against the strains of everyday life.

When I look back to when I started the UK Black Business Show, there were times I wanted to give up; balancing a side hustle with a full-time job and a family was no easy feat, and continuing to pursue something that was not yet lucrative was draining. But whenever I became weary and felt like quitting, it was the community that reminded me why it was so important. How could I stop a show that meant so much to others? It was bigger than just me. I kept going not only because I was passionate about creating a space for Black entrepreneurs and professionals but because so many people needed what I had created, and it felt like taking it away from them would be criminal.

Communities not only enable healthier living through shared activities, they also provide purpose and meaning. Engaging with a community, whether through volunteering, participating in group activities or contributing to collective goals, offers individuals a sense of identity and values. It helps combat feelings of isolation and disconnection, and provides a reason to wake up each day with a sense of affinity and direction.

Collective Wisdom

Another reason why communities are so powerful is the collective wisdom they offer. At an individual level, shared networks provide access to a wealth of experience, knowledge and guidance. Through social interactions within a group, individuals gather insights and perspectives that they might not have encountered otherwise. This wisdom is not confined to academic or formal education; it extends to practical skills, life lessons and diverse perspectives accumulated from different walks of life. By tapping into collective knowledge, individuals are better equipped to navigate challenges and make informed decisions in both their personal and professional lives.

Professionally, there are many invaluable networks that enable growth and provide opportunity. Whether an association, an industry-specific network or a mentorship programme, these communities offer a platform for professional development. They provide access to resources, opportunities for learning and space for innovation. The exchange of ideas and expertise often leads to career advancements, entrepreneurial ventures and the establishment of mutually beneficial partnerships. Networking within these groups is fertile ground for career progression and success, offering access to a multitude of connections and potential collaborators.

Resilience, both personal and professional, is a cornerstone of a strong community. During challenging times, be it economic downturns, personal crises or professional setbacks, individuals within a community can find a wellspring of support and encouragement. The collective experiences and diverse perspectives offer an array of coping mechanisms and solutions. The communal strength acts as a safety net, providing individuals with guidance, emotional support and practical assistance, enabling them to weather storms with greater ease and bounce back from adversity more effectively.

Elizabeth Uviebinené offered further insight into the key factors she believes help foster resilience: 'Shared values are essential for me, as personally it will be hard to connect with others and sustain a sense of community if there is little shared value. When individuals share values, communication tends to be more effective. It becomes easier to convey thoughts, feelings and expectations . . . These values contribute to a deeper understanding of everyone's perspectives, beliefs and priorities. This shared understanding creates empathy, and helps all parties navigate challenges with greater sensitivity when there is conflict.'

Shared values are not just beneficial but necessary for meaningful connections and sustained community cohesion. They facilitate more effective communication, allowing individuals to express thoughts, feelings and expectations more easily. Elizabeth suggests that the strength and the resilience of a community are significantly bolstered by shared values guiding interactions and strengthening bonds.

The resilience of a community often transcends individual resilience. On a broader societal level, communities can band together to face larger challenges and instigate change. Collective efforts within a community can lead to societal resilience – driving improvements, overcoming obstacles and addressing shared concerns. Historically, communities have responded to natural disasters, sociopolitical challenges and public health crises. A community's sense of unity, shared knowledge and collective strength play a crucial role in ensuring societal progress and stability.

And the importance of collective resilience in professional settings is undeniable. Teams that operate in a community-like environment where there is mutual support, shared goals and a culture of cooperation tend to perform better. A sense of belonging and collective responsibility often leads to better choices and increased productivity, and ensures an environment that is conducive to innovation and problem-solving. Companies that have a strong sense of community among their employees benefit from greater engagement, reduced turnover and enhanced overall performance. The supportive atmosphere within these professional contexts fuels creativity and drives organizations toward success.

CHAPTER 2

Building Your Personal Brand through Community

'Personal branding is becoming less of a competitive edge and more of a requirement for anyone looking to grow their business; get that dream job; or take their career to the next level.'

— Ryan Erskine[3]

We've examined the foundation of community, but what role does it play in shaping and amplifying our personal brands? This chapter is all about learning how to leverage relationships and narrate compelling stories in order to stand out in a crowded place and catapult your personal brand.

In a world where connections are currency and relationships fuel success, the concept of creating a strong brand goes beyond self-promotion. Yes, you can showcase your skills and accomplishments, but when you draw others into your story, values and mission, there's no stopping you.

The support, insights and relationships provided by a community can open doors and influence the narrative of your own journey. Understanding the importance of community engagement can help you reach new heights.

Karen Wardle is someone who has utilized the support and insights of others to open doors in her own career. With over twenty years' experience in marketing and events, working in-house for a number of financial institutions as well as at marketing agencies, she has established herself as an expert in the field.

As a leader of teams, Karen is people-focused and passionate about diversity and equality. Strategic and customer-focused in her approach, she also has a strong track record of leading her team in the design and delivery of engaging campaigns that create a lasting impact. When I spoke to her, she had valuable insights to share on how to build an adaptable personal brand and how to show up.

'To grow as a person and to develop, I realized I needed to identify supportive, trusted colleagues and friends who could help me to establish a strong brand that not only fulfilled the need I had today but would help me build my future career goals. It was also important for me to seek input more broadly, so I set about establishing myself in new professional circles where I could learn and observe to gain different perspectives. While I didn't always have my career goals all mapped out, I knew some of the key areas where I wanted to progress. I set about identifying people from within different communities, who were at different stages of their career and could share their experiences from which I could learn. I also wanted to understand my blind spots – being open to feedback enabled me to further define who I wanted to be, be clear on my purpose and stay true to my values.

'Throughout all of my conversations, it was also important to be transparent, so they knew the questions I was asking were relating to me wanting to better understand how I showed up. Being vulnerable and sharing that you are on a journey is important to ensure feedback that is given to you is tailored, thoughtful and relevant. Adopting this approach over the last ten years has helped me be successful in my chosen career path through securing promotions and opportunities that, without the input of my network, may not have been possible to achieve.'

Building a community grounded in transparency is critical to the evolution and refinement of your personal brand. Karen's approach – actively seeking out a network of colleagues and friends and immersing herself in new professional communities to gain diverse perspectives – is a strategic and introspective method.

Karen recognized that building a brand is not a static endeavour but a process that evolves alongside your career and personal growth. She identified and engaged with individuals at different stages of their careers, enriching her development of her own career trajectory.

Your branding must be intentional. You need to decide how you will present yourself to people – a personal brand is all about visibility and the values that you outwardly represent. Your brand contains all the content that's available about you as a person, and once you have built your personal brand, it is very hard to change it once that identity is set.[4]

I've been fortunate enough to have been featured on esteemed platforms like *Forbes*, *The Times*, the *Telegraph*, Sky News, the BBC, the *Evening Standard*, *Stylist* and more. Of course, this is a significant achievement, but it is not only reflective of my individual success. It was through the backing, encouragement and engagement of my community that I gained traction and recognition, and for that I'll always be grateful.

Kanya King MBE is the founder of MOBO, the largest urban music awards organization in Europe. Kanya is living proof of the old adage that a genuine leader moulds rather than seeks consensus. An internationally renowned entrepreneur, and a CEO, founder and visionary, Kanya displayed the rare drive and ambition necessary to help take Black music from something produced by disenfranchised artists at the margins of British popular culture to the heart of the mainstream in the UK.

She told me: 'Surrounding yourself with positive, driven people can significantly impact your journey. Role models and networks in your community, family or friends offer opportunities for networking, learning and visibility, all essential for building a strong and authentic personal brand.'

When you are surrounded by individuals who are positive and goal-oriented, it naturally propels you forward, forging your path and shaping how others perceive you. Role models, wherever they come from, play a crucial role in this process. They not only serve as sources of inspiration through their own achievements and attitudes, but also help to open up avenues.

Indie Gordon is a multi-award-winning entrepreneur, government consultant and global coach. She told me about a recent stand-out moment in her journey to becoming a Forty Under 40 Awards UK recipient: 'To be honest, I hadn't considered applying for it. It was my community that saw the opportunity, nominated me, and even had someone from the community present me with the honour. It's incredible how a group of like-minded people can spot opportunities you might overlook. The Forty Under 40 Award was life-changing, adding a layer to my brand that I didn't realize I needed.'

The award was a significant milestone for Indie. It served as a public acknowledgement of her contributions and impact, enhanced her credibility, standing and stature in her field, opened new doors for professional opportunities and furthered her influence.

This illustrates a fundamental aspect that is often overlooked: the role of your community as both a supporter and an active participant in your journey. Indie's story shows the benefit of having people behind you who not only provide support and encouragement but also actively seek and identify opportunities for recognition that you might not pursue on your own.

There are countless individuals out there who have used their connections to get recommendations and opportunities. When you focus on building meaningful relationships, you can change the way people see and recognize you, and create a powerful and influential personal brand.

Leveraging Community Connections

To leverage means 'to use something that you already have in order to achieve something new or better'.[5] Usually, people talk about a community and a personal brand separately, but they can and should be talked about together.

The truth is that anyone who is successful has relied on the backing of a support group. How do they accomplish this? It all begins with networking and developing strong relationships. As these relationships grow and solidify, the composition of a network becomes pivotal. To ensure a thriving network, there needs to be diversity. And engagement is vital, not only with individuals from your professional domain but also across broader groups of people who share your passions, hobbies and personal interests.

Continuously connecting with people from different backgrounds and those who have different experiences from you can offer fresh insights and unexpected opportunities. 'Cultural sensitivity' is significant, and embracing other cultures will expand your horizons, allowing you to absorb new knowledge, become more open-minded, and perceive things from diverse viewpoints. If you possess the ability to navigate different cultures, you will be empowered to build a formidable brand rooted in connections to a range of groups.[6]

It's important to note though that leveraging relationships is impossible without authenticity. Having genuine connections with those you engage with is essential. The detrimental ramifications of perceived inauthenticity cannot be overstated. The foundation of your character is built upon reputation and word-of-mouth. Thus, ensuring authenticity becomes the differentiating factor between establishing a robust brand and one that is much more prone to collapsing under pressure. Unless someone personally knows you, it is very likely that they will form an opinion about you based on either their interpretation of what you have put out into the world or what other people have said about you. According to an article in *Forbes*, 92 per cent of people trust recommendations from other people (even if they don't know them) over brands.[7] This is why it is imperative for you to create strong, authentic connections.

So, what characterizes an authentic relationship? How do you genuinely initiate connection with others? Authentic connection-building entails engaging in sincere conversations without preconceived intentions of personal gain.

Kerry Griffith advises business leaders on inclusive leadership and equity in the workplace, helping businesses to identify their most intractable inclusion challenges and allowing them to drive positive change and reap the benefits of a welcoming workplace culture. He discussed the practices he's adopted to ensure authenticity in his relationships, which he believes has had a huge impact on how he is perceived.

'In the quest for authentic relationships, I've discovered that practising authenticity in every interaction is key. It's not as straightforward as it sounds, though. We're often aware that our intended impression may not always align with how others perceive us, leading us to subtly adjust ourselves to be received more favourably. This desire to fit in and to feel included is a natural part of the human condition. It is particularly evident in team dynamics and professional settings, where how you present and how you are perceived can significantly impact future success. Why wouldn't you present your best self?

'A pivotal moment for me came when a trusted colleague offered three simple words of advice: "Be more you." This insight highlighted how I sometimes held back in certain interactions, and the impact it had. I put some of this down to code-switching. These character changes can occasionally make a person appear inauthentic. Those three words became a catalyst for change. I realized the importance of being emotionally and intellectually consistent and having someone in your corner, willing to be a mirror. This lesson extends beyond the professional realm and proves invaluable in personal relationships.

'I frequently revisit those three words, which have come to signify authenticity, sound judgement and empathy, to ensure my presence aligns with these principles. This commitment echoes in my career choices, where authenticity and inclusive leadership are paramount. My brand reflects these principles, influencing not only my professional journey but also how I guide others to embrace their own authenticity.'

Kerry's insight highlights a universal challenge: the tension between presenting yourself in a manner that you hope is favourably received and the inherent desire to remain true to your authentic self. This tension is magnified in professional settings, where impressions can have a direct impact on career progression and success.

Authenticity goes beyond honesty or transparency; it encompasses emotional and intellectual consistency across different facets of your life. Consistency is crucial in developing a brand synonymous with authenticity and integrity.

Kerry also touched on the concept of code-switching, acknowledging the complexities of navigating different social and professional contexts while striving to maintain authenticity. This adaptability, while often necessary, can sometimes come at the cost of appearing inauthentic, thereby hindering the development of trust and genuine connections within your community.

Kerry's commitment to the principles of authenticity, sound judgement and empathy, and his emphasis on inclusive leadership, reflect a deep understanding of the role these values play. By aligning your professional demeanour and decisions with these core values, you will not only navigate your career path with integrity but also become an example for others seeking to embrace their own sense of authenticity.

Kerry's words beautifully illustrate that at the heart of effective personal branding is the courage to be yourself, fully and unapologetically. Khalia Ismain also highlighted the importance of these values. Khalia is the founder of Jamii, an online marketplace and discovery platform for Black creators and makers in the UK. Launched in 2016, Jamii is now home to over 250 makers and small brands, and has organically grown a community of more than 38,000 people keen to align their purchases with purpose. Named as one of *Cosmopolitan* magazine's 'Positivity Index: 24 People (Genuinely) Making the World a Better

Place' in 2021, she is on a mission to make shopping with community-owned businesses as easy as possible.

In November 2022, Khalia took a role as the Black Entrepreneurs Programme Manager at Lloyds Banking Group, utilizing the resources and influence of one of the country's biggest banks to effect systemic change for Black businesses. In this position, she has led the Black in Business partnership with Channel 4, providing five Black-owned businesses with £100,000 worth of TV advertising each, as well as initiatives that have provided over 20,000 hours of support to more than 5,000 Black entrepreneurs. But what might be even more impressive is that Khalia was a first-time founder straight out of university, with no previous experience in business.

'For me to be successful, I recognized how crucial it would be for me to build relationships with founders who were further along in their journey, and who would be willing to share their experience and wisdom with me,' she told me. 'To ensure authenticity in my relationships, I leaned into being authentically me – I am naturally warm and friendly, inquisitive about other people's journeys, and open and willing to share my own. I sought to create long-term, enjoyable and mutually beneficial connections and avoided "networking" in the traditional sense. This has led to people feeling comfortable in asking me for support, and simultaneously they are keen to support me – which has resulted in introductions, opportunities and visibility that I would never have been able to achieve alone.'

Khalia's story of launching Jamii as a first-time founder shows the importance of genuine connections over transactional networking, particularly in the early stages of establishing a business. By prioritizing authenticity in her interactions, Khalia tapped into her inherent traits of warmth and friendliness, curiosity about others, and openness in sharing her personal experiences. Her approach to building relationships is noteworthy in its departure from traditional networking, which can often feel superficial or opportunistic. The focus on creating long-term, enjoyable and mutually beneficial connections speaks to a deeper understanding of relationship-building as a reciprocal exchange of value.

Khalia's strategy of seeking out more experienced founders for guidance and wisdom, while offering her own support and enthusiasm in return, created relationships based on genuine interest and mutual respect. This authenticity in relationship-building not only facilitated a comfortable environment for exchanging support, but also led to significant opportunities and increased visibility for Jamii that might not have been accessible otherwise. Her success with this approach demonstrates the power of authentic relationships in the entrepreneurial ecosystem. Such relationships can open doors to introductions and opportunities far beyond the reach of traditional networking efforts.

Community-building encourages us to consider the impact of our actions beyond immediate gains. It invites introspection about the nature of our contributions, helps to build a reputation founded on trust, and paves the way for an ecosystem in which teamwork flourishes organically.

What is truly fascinating is the ripple effect of generosity. Embracing a mindset of selfless contribution sets the stage for a culture steeped in benevolence. Individuals who have an ethos of giving without immediate expectations will form a network where reciprocal actions become the norm, creating a supportive environment that propels collective growth.

By imparting knowledge generously, endorsing other endeavours and offering constructive feedback, you position yourself not as a mere participant but as an active stalwart of support. This virtuous cycle often leads to organic recognition, collaborative ventures and unforeseen opportunities that stem from the goodwill you've shown to others.

I've connected with so many people throughout my career as a working professional and entrepreneur. I have gained countless opportunities through people who I connected with initially on a friendship basis. What always touches me are the kind words that I hear about myself, and I put this down to having genuine authentic relationships with others. I've done things for people without expecting anything back – and sometimes you may never get anything back, and that's OK. But I assure you that the more you give, the more you will receive.

There are so many ways you can give, whether it's your time, expertise or even facilitating a useful connection. I want to challenge you to embrace the opportunity to contribute, knowing that each instance of offering guidance or assistance is a brushstroke on the canvas of your good reputation – creating a masterpiece that echoes your commitment to the collective growth of your community and defining your enduring legacy within it.

Social Media Platforms

Online and offline platforms play a key part in building your personal brand. Whether social media, forums, industry-specific groups, local meet-ups or professional events, each platform presents unique opportunities. By understanding how to navigate these spaces effectively, you can significantly elevate your visibility, credibility and impact.

In today's digital world, social media is a great place to build your brand. Different platforms offer unique ways to do this. For instance, LinkedIn is great for professional networking and sharing your knowledge. X (formerly Twitter) is good for short messages and using hashtags to connect with people and build a following. Instagram lets you tell your story through visuals, showing off your personality and skills. Facebook's groups help you connect with others in your industry, in order to share knowledge. To stand out, it's important to adapt your approach to each platform, and use their special features to tell your brand's story in a consistent way.

Stefan Johnson provided some insight on how he balances online and offline networking. A video producer and trade finance director from South-East London, Stefan discovered his passion for media in 2004 after being challenged by his English teacher Ms Hadley-Stone.

Stefan chose to study media because he thought it would be fun. For a project, he made a video with his best friend, but when they showed it in class, they received negative feedback from the teacher because it wasn't very good. Challenged to try again, Stefan and his friend worked hard to make a better video. This time, Ms Hadley-Stone loved it, and they got a lot of praise. She told them she'd always known what they were capable of, which is why she'd been so tough on them at first. That moment was a game-changer for Stefan. It's when he really fell in love with media and started to feel passionate about it.

Stefan went on to graduate with a distinction in Media Production, gained a bachelor's degree in Broadcasting Content and Creation, and founded Simply Justified Productions (SJP) in 2008, aimed at empowering entrepreneurs through impactful video content. SJP subsequently helped establish figures like TV and radio presenter Remel London and sales entrepreneur Trist Taylor, who inspires others on their personal development journeys via the motivational platform GrowDaily.

Keen to understand what makes a good business great, in 2014 Stefan added corporate finance to his skill set, incrementally rising from bank cashier to a senior role as HSBC Trade Finance Director. Despite having no formal financial qualifications, he supported hundreds of small and midsized enterprises (SMEs) with millions in order to fund their growth plans.

To Stefan, 'balancing online and offline networking is akin to navigating the world of dating' – although he has been married for many years and admits he's rusty on the concept! Nonetheless, he says that 'in both realms, the emphasis is on quality connections rather than simply collecting contacts like kids collecting Pokémon cards. A pet peeve of mine is when individuals randomly bulk-connect with people (for instance on LinkedIn) for the sake of racking up volume, but forgetting the importance of value.

'You should engage in virtual conversations with finesse, attending webinars, participating in forums and dropping insightful comments. But don't forget the importance of face-to-face interactions at conferences and local meet-ups (the infamous coffee chat) for that personal touch.

'It's important to vary your communication methods, just as in dating, using thoughtful texts for online engagement and meaningful calls for offline interactions. The mix between group events and solo efforts ensures a well-rounded networking approach – networking is a mix of connection and engagement that contributes greatly to professional success.

'In a world where connections are easily made and forgotten, the extra effort of in-person networking stands out, making you memorable. I have experienced the benefits of this myself – senior stakeholders seeing my interpersonal skills as I "work a room" of managing directors, clients and prospects, directly helped my career. Speaking to sponsors and advocates later, they would pinpoint events or seminars where they witnessed how I carried myself in-person as a defining factor of my personal and professional brand.

'The unique benefits of in-person networking are often underestimated in our hyper-connected digital age. Eye contact, firm handshakes and non-verbal cues convey confidence, trust and sincerity, providing a depth that virtual exchanges often lack.'

Stefan offers an interesting perspective on the interplay between online and offline networking, drawing an apt comparison to the world of dating to emphasize the importance of quality over quantity in building connections. We should be establishing meaningful relationships rather than amassing a large number of superficial contacts. Just as in personal relationships, long-term success depends on the depth and quality of our professional connections.

Florence Henderson is the Inclusion lead for Europe, Middle East and Africa at Moody's. She is responsible for advancing Moody's commitment to Inclusion by implementing strategic initiatives to attract, retain and promote a diverse workforce and create an equitable and inclusive environment for all employees. Her role also includes senior stakeholder management, project management, coordinating Business Resource Groups (BRGs), communications, and oversight of improvements in benchmarking and advancement of Moody's Inclusion goals.

Florence was once told by one of her previous managers that she needed to build her personal brand – but she wasn't quite sure what that meant at the time. 'Conversations with another ex-manager, who I had asked to support me as an executive sponsor as part of a talent programme, really helped me define what that meant for myself. He spoke to me about my network (or community) that I was building on LinkedIn. He asked how I was leveraging that community – beyond just connecting with people and liking a few comments. Speaking with him helped me see that this network or community could help with creating meaningful relationships that could be beneficial not only to them, but to me too, opening doors to speaking engagements, business leads and future roles.'

There is untapped potential within your network to support personal and professional growth. The key to unlocking this potential lies in actively engaging with the community – sharing insights, contributing to discussions and offering value, whether offline or online. Proactive engagement can transform a static network into a dynamic community.

Florence's experience also highlights the importance of mentorship and guidance. The conversation with her executive sponsor acted as a catalyst for a strategic re-evaluation of how to use social media effectively for brand-building. Asking for perspective from external stakeholders and mentors can play a huge role in uncovering the strategic value of your network, and leveraging it to achieve professional objectives.

Online connections undoubtedly cast a wide net, allowing individuals to engage with a global audience, amplify their reach and facilitate initial introductions. However, the essence lies not just in visibility but in forging enduring, authentic relationships. It's about transcending the superficiality of digital likes and follows to create a tapestry of trust and mutual respect that can only be woven through real-world encounters.

Networking Events

Consider the symphony of networking events, industry conferences and local meet-ups – a melting pot of diverse minds converging to exchange ideas and forge connections.

Here, beyond avatars and profile pictures, individuals have the chance to witness body language, subtle cues and genuine expressions that can be the bedrock of establishing a rapport and credibility.

In my own career, these events allowed me the opportunity to connect with peers, industry leaders, potential clients and sponsors. I actively engaged in conversations, exchanged business cards and phone numbers, and added people on LinkedIn. What I didn't expect was to make friends who are still a part of my community today and who have supported me on my entrepreneurial journey.

I had the chance to chat with the head of a huge tech company while we were backstage at one event, and she talked about how getting ahead in your career is like a 'hidden game'. She stressed that knowing the right people is key – even more important than what you're taught on your career journey.

Making solid connections through networking doesn't just help you get jobs, it helps you find sponsors, mentors and exciting new projects. It also shapes how others see you professionally. Your relationships with people in your circle reflect who you are as a professional. When these connections vouch for you or give positive feedback, it really impacts how others view you at work. Building trust and being seen as reliable are huge benefits of these relationships.

Do you think that in advancing your career and understanding this 'hidden game' – navigating networks and forming meaningful connections – is as important as, or maybe even more important than, just having the right skills and knowledge? I do.

In-person networking is an arena where serendipity thrives. It might be an unexpected conversation in the lift, a chance encounter during a break, or a shared moment of insight at a panel discussion. These moments go beyond the scripted nature of online interactions, allowing the spontaneity and depth that can catalyse powerful lasting relationships.

When you think of it, online networking acts as the first brushstrokes, painting the background of visibility and initial introductions. However, it's the finer brushstrokes of in-person connections that add depth, colour and texture to the canvas. They provide the intricate details that bring your story to life, creating meaningful relationships that endure beyond the transient nature of digital interactions.

While the digital landscape offers immense potential, the significance of in-person networking cannot be overstated. It's about finding a harmonious balance between the convenience of online reach and the impact of face-to-face conversations. Embracing both realms creates a holistic approach – one that not only amplifies visibility but also cultivates a network of genuine, lasting connections founded on trust, authenticity and shared experiences.

Consistent Engagement

According to an article in *Forbes*, 'it takes five to seven impressions for someone to remember a brand'.[8] Consistency is the key to leveraging your networks effectively. It's not merely about occasional participation but rather an ongoing, deliberate effort that reaps significant benefits. Here's why consistent engagement matters in leveraging communities.

Establishing Presence

What is presence? It's hard to define, but just like love, people know when they feel it. You can see someone who has presence just like you can see a couple and know they are so in love. But I'll try to define it simply: to have presence, you must be present.

Regular and consistent engagement helps establish your presence within a community. Being consistently active keeps you on people's radars, making you a familiar and recognizable figure. This visibility is essential for brand recognition.

Building Trust and Credibility

Consistency breeds trust. By consistently engaging and contributing valuable insights or assistance, you establish credibility within a community. When your actions consistently align with your words, when you deliver on promises and when your conduct reflects integrity and reliability, trust begins to form. Credibility, on the other hand, stems from expertise, consistency and a track record of success. When others recognize your knowledge, reliability and consistent performance, your credibility grows.

Deepening Connections

Building meaningful relationships takes time and persistence. Consistent engagement allows you to forge deeper connections with other community members. This will go a long way in cementing your brand within the community's collective consciousness. These deeper connections are built on mutual respect, shared values and genuine care, allowing you to showcase your authenticity and values. Actively participating in initiatives, offering support and contributing your skills not only enriches the lives of those around you but also positions you as an integral part of the communal fabric.

Showcasing Reliability

Regular participation showcases your reliability. It demonstrates that you are committed and dependable, which are essential traits for a strong personal brand. It's not just about what you say, it's about being there to contribute and assist actively. Fulfilling commitments, being dependable and delivering on promises contribute significantly to how you are perceived by others. When you always show up and follow through on your word, whether it's by volunteering, assisting others or being a reliable team member, you establish a reputation for trustworthiness. As word spreads about your reliability, it becomes a defining factor in how others perceive and trust you. Ultimately, this solidifies your reputation as someone dependable, competent and integral within your community and professional circles.

Opportunity for Learning and Growth

Consistent engagement isn't just about what you give; it's also about what you gain. Regularly engaging exposes you to new perspectives and insights, enabling continuous learning and personal growth. This growth will reflect positively on your brand. Actively seeking out chances to expand your knowledge, develop new skills and contribute to the community's betterment not only benefits you personally but also bolsters your reputation.

Staying Topical and Relevant

Communities evolve and discussions shift over time. Consistent engagement allows you to stay up-to-date and relevant within the community. It enables you to align your contributions with current trends and ongoing conversations, keeping your brand fresh and pertinent. Staying abreast of current events, industry trends and interests positions you as an informed and engaged individual. By consistently contributing relevant and timely information, whether through social media, public forums or local in-person events, you establish yourself as a trusted source and a go-to person within your niche.

Solidifying Influence

Building influence is gradual, and it's nurtured through consistent engagement. Over time, your presence and valuable contributions will position you as an authority.

In essence, consistent engagement within communities isn't just about being present; it's about actively nurturing relationships, showcasing expertise and demonstrating a commitment to mutual growth. It's the foundation upon which a compelling and influential brand is constructed within these interconnected networks. By actively taking on community leadership roles, initiating impactful projects or mentoring others, you establish yourself as a respected figure.

Being part of the Scotland Women in Technology community for many years and taking on a leadership role within that community was incredibly impactful to Lynsey Campbell's personal brand. 'I always had a natural passion for equality and inclusion but being able to demonstrate that and showcase my passion to a much wider and more diverse audience meant that I began to be known for those values and that also helped shape my career as a respected people leader.'

By Lynsey actively participating in the community, she not only engaged with her passion for equality and inclusion but also leveraged this platform to amplify her voice and extend her influence. The leadership position within such a focused community allowed Lynsey a unique opportunity to demonstrate commitment and expertise in areas that are critically important in today's professional landscape. Her active involvement showcases the power of aligning personal passions with professional roles, and the impact this alignment can have.

Being recognized for your contributions to important causes like equality and inclusion can significantly enhance your credibility and gain you respect as a leader. This recognition goes beyond mere acknowledgement of leadership skills, extending to a deep appreciation of your commitment to making a difference within your community and industry.

Taking on roles that align with your values can serve as a powerful mechanism for becoming a respected and influential person. Engaging, particularly in leadership capacities, can propel your career forward by establishing you as a credible and respected voice in your areas of passion and expertise.

Following Up and Nurturing Relationships

By building on your networking and relationship-building, you can better understand the strategies and approaches necessary to establish and maintain strong, meaningful connections. This, in turn, contributes significantly to your standing within these networks.

Regular Communication

Stay in touch with your connections using various communication channels such as emails, calls, social media messages or in-person meet-ups (if possible). Ensure your messages are personalized and not solely about your needs. Make sure to inquire about the other person's well-being, share updates about your own ventures, and express genuine interest in their activities. Consistent communication shows that you value the relationship and keeps the connection active.

Provide Relevant Updates

Share periodic updates about your work, achievements, projects, or any other valuable content that might benefit your connections. This demonstrates your willingness to share knowledge and keeps them informed about your progress, reinforcing your credibility and expertise. However, focus on sharing information that aligns with their interests or could be useful to them.

Add Value to the Relationship

Continuously seek ways to add value to your connections. This could involve sharing articles, resources or insights that are relevant to their interests or profession. Offer assistance or support when needed, provide introductions to other valuable contacts, or collaborate on projects if such opportunities arise. By being helpful and supportive, you will establish yourself as a reliable and valuable connection.

Opportunities Through Connections

Andy Ayim MBE is a living example of how connections can lead to job offers – and even to meeting influential people like President Obama. 'In 2017, as an experienced blogger, I shared hundreds of stories about diversity and inclusion in the technology sector to highlight relevant role models from underrepresented backgrounds,' he told me. 'In a change of pace, I decided I wanted to start a podcast and take a break from blogging, so I reached out to various role models for interviews as part of the podcast series. One of those individuals was a lady called Arlan Hamilton, founding partner of Backstage Capital. Her story is one of resilience and a determination to create a $10m venture capital fund to invest in people from the LGBTQ+ community, women and people of colour.

'We had a riveting conversation, so I decided to invite her to the UK to experience the shared inequalities she was addressing in the US. The trip was fantastic as we met with a range of ecosystem players from academics to investors and founders. At the end of the trip, during a meeting at a VC's office, she surprised me by offering me the job of managing director for her new brainchild, a start-up accelerator programme.

'We went on to raise $2.5m, review nearly 2,000 founder applications and invest $100,000 into twenty-five start-ups led by underrepresented founders across the global accelerator programme in London, Detroit, LA and Philadelphia. This helped position me as a key person of influence for diversity in the technology sector and eventually led me to meet key figures like former president Obama, and I received a Member of the Most Excellent Order of the British Empire (MBE) from the Royal Family for my contributions to the technology sector in the UK.'

Andy made a strategic pivot when he launched his podcast, and this set the stage for an encounter with a notable figure in venture capital. This choice to engage directly with influential role models through a new medium not only broadened his reach but also deepened his engagement with key issues and personalities in the sector.

The sequence of events after Andy invited Arlan Hamilton to visit the UK illustrates the power of initiative and the creation of opportunities through proactive outreach. The visit facilitated valuable exchanges with various ecosystem players, showcasing his role as a connector and enabler within the tech community. The unexpected job offer that these engagements culminated in shows the serendipitous nature of opportunities that can arise from building and nurturing connections.

Andy's story highlights several key insights about the value of connections:

- *Proactive engagement*: Reaching out to established figures can open doors to new opportunities.
- *Strategic visibility*: Shifting mediums or platforms can rejuvenate your approach and attract attention in influential circles.
- *The ripple effect*: Initial connections can lead to a cascade of opportunities, amplifying your impact and influence far beyond the original scope of your work.
- *Recognition and influence*: Sustained contributions to a field, facilitated by strategic networking, can lead to significant accolades and recognition.

Making connections isn't just about swapping business cards or adding each other on LinkedIn. The real power comes from building genuine relationships over time. It's like tending to a garden of diverse minds, where each person brings a different view. This mix of ideas creates a fertile ground for creativity.

Value Exchange and Contribution

A community relies on its members exchanging value and making contributions. Exploring this further helps us to understand the essential dynamics that support the development and continuity of a personal brand within a community system.

The core of value exchange is being real and sincere. It's not just about showing kindness in order to gain something in return. It's about genuinely giving something valuable to a community without expecting an immediate pay-off. This builds trust and credibility, and provides a strong foundation.

Understanding what a community truly needs is vital for effective value exchange. It means really listening and empathizing with the struggles and goals of others. By matching your contributions to these needs and using your particular skills or passions, you can provide value that will connect you with your community.

Jamelia Donaldson shared with me her experiences of understanding what a community needed and creating something to meet this need. 'Establishing the Teen Experience – personal development workshops for Black and mixed-race teenage girls aged 12–19 – has yielded unexpected and substantial personal and professional gains. When we launched the programme in 2018, my primary motivation was not personal gain but rather the genuine desire to enhance the lives of young girls and women, offering them a sense of belonging that may be lacking in their families, schools or social circles.

'The dividends from this community work have been significant. It's easy to forget the far-reaching impact that community initiatives can have, and the unexpected doors they can open. To my surprise, my name has been mentioned in numerous rooms, and parents of the girls touched by the Teen Experience continue to speak highly of the programme. Their acknowledgement has translated into unforeseen opportunities as they put me forward for various professional endeavours.

'The Teen Experience, designed to impart life skills, professional skills and practical know-how, added another dimension to TreasureTress. It showcased that our initiative extends beyond being just a beauty box; it's a movement. The genuine intention to make a positive difference in the lives of others has created a ripple effect that goes beyond the initial scope of the Teen Experience.

'This experience serves as a testament to the notion that when you engage in meaningful community work with the intention of doing good, unexpected but positive outcomes often follow. Seven years later, the recognition and support from the parents and the community itself have not only enriched the lives of the young girls involved but have also, unexpectedly, opened doors for personal and professional growth in my own journey.'

Contribution isn't just about taking part; it's about actively engaging and making a meaningful difference in the community. This could mean sharing unique ideas, solving problems, offering support, or inspiring others by telling your real story in a way that connects with them.

The intention behind your actions plays a crucial role in the value exchange process. Jamelia's primary motivation for launching the Teen Experience was to offer support, guidance and acceptance to a demographic that felt under-served and overlooked. This selfless intention, rooted in a desire to contribute meaningfully to a community, built the foundation for a significant and reciprocal value exchange.

The unexpected personal and professional gains that followed – recognition, respect and new opportunities – demonstrate how contributions to a community can reverberate beyond the immediate impact. The positive feedback and advocacy from parents and the broader community not only elevated the visibility of the Teen Experience but also enhanced Jamelia's personal brand. This progression from community service to professional advancement exemplifies how authentic, meaningful engagement can lead to unforeseen benefits.

The Teen Experience added a new dimension to the broader initiative, reinforcing the idea that value contribution can significantly improve the perception and impact of your endeavours. By extending beyond its initial offering, the initiative showcased the power of a movement driven by genuine care and a commitment to making a difference.

Actively engaging in community work, with the intention of contributing positively, can yield a rich exchange of value. It not only enriches the lives of those served but also creates personal and professional growth for those who serve. When individuals invest their time, resources and energy into making a meaningful difference, the community responds in kind, often in ways that surpass expectations.

Remel London is one of the most exciting breakout names in British broadcasting. Already the face of Sky One's *What's Up TV* and having hosted her own radio show on Capital Xtra for a number of years, Remel is also the founder of much-celebrated creative platform The Mainstream, which provides key networking opportunities, holds live events and workshops/seminars, and produces podcasts in order to help exceptional diverse talent to develop their career in the mainstream media space.

Remel spoke to me about her experience in supporting the community and how that has benefited her professionally. 'I launched The Mainstream in 2017. Back then it was a single-event format where I hosted an in-depth conversation in front of an audience with the rising star and presenter AJ Odudu. On the night, AJ shared her journey into the creative industry, and together with the attendees we stayed for networking. I knew there were creatives following in both of our footsteps, trying to get into the media, TV and film industries, who simply had questions that I felt I alone couldn't answer. I've always known that everyone's journey into the creative industry is different, so I wanted to provide an opportunity to share stories and offer advice in an intimate setting.

'Fast-forward to 2020 and beyond, I was inspired to continue this format as a podcast series, which has seen the likes of Clara Amfo, Mo Gilligan, Dev Griffin, Jimmy Akingbola, London Hughes and Vick Hope, to name a few, share their stories. The podcast has grown and developed into a creative platform which has been recognized by brands such as Prime Video, Sky, the BBC, ITV, Paramount UK, Warner Bros and more as a reputable publication, showcasing and supporting new, existing and high-profile talent in TV and film on a global scale, covering and attending press junkets, screenings and premieres while sharing tips, providing behind-the-scenes access and advice, as well as work experience opportunities for those in our community.'

Launching The Mainstream as a platform for in-depth conversations with industry figures marked the beginning of Remel's journey focusing on sharing diverse pathways into the media, TV and film. The initial event, designed to facilitate networking and advice-sharing, set a precedent for a community-centric initiative aimed at supporting aspiring creatives.

Starting a podcast as part of The Mainstream's platform expanded her reach and impact, and this transition shows the importance of adaptability and innovation when it comes to shaping a personal brand. By providing a mix of inspirational stories, practical advice and behind-the-scenes access, the podcast has become a significant resource for those looking to break into or navigate the creative industry.

Contributing to the community means using your strengths and passions to make it better. It's not just about promoting yourself; it's about genuinely wanting to help the community grow. When you contribute honestly, it creates a chain reaction and encourages others to work together and support each other.

Consistency is key in making a lasting impact. Contributing is an ongoing effort that needs dedication over time. By continuously adding value and genuinely giving, you establish a cycle where trust and respect naturally grow.

In short, contributing to a community is about building relationships and creating an atmosphere where everyone helps each other, benefiting both your personal brand and the community as a whole.

Alignment with Community Values

Crafting a personal brand within a community isn't just about standing out; it's about integrating seamlessly into the community's values and principles. This alignment holds the key to establishing a compelling and enduring presence within your community.

Consider the dynamism of communities – they evolve, adapt and redefine their values over time. You need to adjust and grow alongside them while remaining attuned to the evolving pulse of the community, demonstrating a commitment to its progress and development.

Reciprocity plays a vital role. How do your contributions to the community reflect an understanding of its needs and aspirations? Are you adding substantial value through your unique skills, insights or resources, thereby strengthening the fabric of the community?

Consider the ripple effect of alignment. How might your aligned personal brand positively influence others? And in what ways can you become an advocate, catalyst or contributor to the community's growth and prosperity?

Visibility and Thought Leadership

Visibility acts as the initial gateway to establishing yourself within a community. How effectively are you utilizing various platforms, both online and offline, to amplify your presence within a community? You must engage consistently and authentically to ensure your brand remains visible and recognizable.

Visibility alone isn't sufficient, however – it's the substance behind it that truly defines your influence. This is where thought leadership comes into play. Are your actions, messages and contributions aligned authentically with your personal brand, and is your visibility based on substance and authenticity rather than mere self-promotion or surface-level engagement?

Thought leadership requires a deep understanding of your niche. Are you staying up-to-date on the latest trends, advancements and discussions within your field? Can you constantly hone your expertise and knowledge to become a go-to resource within your community?

Moreover, think about your approach to thought leadership. Are you initiating meaningful conversations, challenging existing norms, or providing solutions to pertinent issues within the community? It's imperative you start to contribute intellectually and practically, to elevate the discourse and encourage progress within your sphere of influence.

As a thought leader, can you influence your community's perceptions, discussions and decisions? Thought leaders have the ability to drive positive change or innovation.

Consider the longevity of your visibility and thought leadership. How will you sustain and improve your visibility while consistently offering valuable insights and perspectives? Can you maintain thought leadership by adapting to changes in your field and remaining ahead of the curve?

Integrating yourself into your workplace community can significantly boost your visibility within your company. This visibility is not just about being seen, it's about being recognized for your unique skills and valuable contributions.

When you're actively involved in a community, you're not just a face in the crowd; you become a known entity, someone whose ideas and input are sought after and respected.

Research lends empirical weight to this observation, and studies have found that individuals who are well connected within their company are more likely to have their ideas approved. This further validates the power of community to elevate an individual's influence and credibility within an organization.

The creation of a personal brand within a community is not just about being visible, it's about being consistently associated with positive traits such as expertise, reliability and leadership. A positive reputation can open doors to career advancement opportunities – such as promotions and leadership roles – that might otherwise remain closed.

Think of visibility and thought leadership as catalysts for personal brand development within a community. How does a balance between visibility and substance contribute to establishing a compelling and influential presence? How might your thought leadership shape not only your personal brand, but also the collective intellect, growth and direction of your community?

What's Your Compelling Narrative?

Crafting a compelling narrative is an art that goes beyond storytelling. Your narrative is how others perceive and connect with your brand.

Consider the essence of your narrative. How effectively are you communicating your personal-brand story to the community? Are you authentically showcasing who you are and what you stand for in a way that aligns with that community's values and interests?

Reflect on the emotional resonance of your narrative within the community. Your brand story needs to evoke emotions, empathy or relatability. Are you creating a narrative that touches upon shared experiences or aspirations?

In addition to this, think about how to further embed authenticity in your narrative. Is your brand story genuine, transparent and consistent with your actions and contributions? How are you aligning your narrative with your values and beliefs and the community's ethos, to establish credibility and trust?

Cecil Peters is an acclaimed thought leader on the role of diversity and inclusion in strengthening communities. He is the EMEA (Europe, Middle East and Africa) Head of Diversity, Equity and Inclusion at JPMorgan Chase & Co., having joined the company as a banking technologist to run a software engineering function with cybersecurity in 2018. During the pandemic he pivoted in his career to focus full-time on diversity, equity and inclusion across JPMorgan's EMEA business, encompassing thirty-six countries and 30,000 employees. He spoke to me about how he shared his narrative authentically and how it in turn created opportunities for others to learn.

'It took me many years before I was comfortable sharing my personal brand story in a professional setting. Yes, when I was with my friends, those with similar backgrounds – either ethnic or socio-economic – we could speak our truth. But rarely for most of my working life was there space to really tell my story in a professional setting. That was until I came to JPMorgan Chase, where they fought so hard to hire me from my previous company, I felt they needed to know what they were getting.

'So I spoke my story to anyone that wanted to listen. I found that the audience was wide and went deep. From senior managing directors that wanted help navigating relationships with colleagues from different backgrounds, to students looking for a way to get comfortable in the world of corporate enterprise.

'I was authentic, I spoke about the good and bad that had happened to me, and I spoke about what systemic change would look like. I even shared stories of my daily commute and the seat next to me on public transport often being the last one to be taken. If you are not strong, it could give you a complex. Fortunately the responses were overwhelmingly positive. By sharing simple tips on how to do better, I found I had an audience that was willing to learn. So I went from having no shared personal-brand story to becoming one of a number of spokespersons for a whole community across the City.'

Cecil's initial hesitation to share his story in a professional setting is a common sentiment, reflecting broader societal norms that often compartmentalize professional and personal identities. However, his decision to communicate his personal journey openly at J P Morgan Chase illustrates a critical moment of change, both for him and for the audience he was engaging with.

Sharing personal experiences, particularly those that highlight cultural, ethnic or socio-economic backgrounds, serves multiple purposes. Firstly, it humanizes the professional environment, allowing for a deeper connection between colleagues beyond the surface level of work-related interactions. Secondly, it educates and enlightens others about the diverse experiences of their co-workers, leading to more empathy and understanding within the corporate culture. This can be particularly impactful for senior management, and others who may not have direct exposure to the challenges faced by different demographics within their organization or society at large.

The positive reception to Cecil's story shows the hunger for authentic voices and narratives within corporate spaces. Cecil's openness not only empowered him, it also gave him a platform from which to influence systemic change and advocate for inclusivity – and it benefited those he spoke to, offering them a new perspective and practical advice on creating a more inclusive environment.

Cecil's progression from reluctance to becoming a spokesperson for diversity, equity and inclusion highlights the importance of visibility and representation in professional settings. Strong, authentic narratives can bridge gaps between diverse groups, facilitating a culture of learning, empathy and mutual respect. Cecil's evolution also reflects a shift in corporate culture towards valuing diversity and inclusion not just in policy but in practice, with companies beginning to recognize the unique contributions and insights that come from a multitude of backgrounds.

Now, consider the power of relatability in your own brand story. How are you weaving elements into your narrative that resonate with the challenges, dreams or aspirations of community members? Are you demonstrating empathy and understanding through your narrative, making your brand more approachable and relatable?

Reflect on the impact of your narrative. How does your brand story inspire, motivate or empower others? In what ways does your narrative drive engagement and encourage others to align with your vision or mission?

Think about the evolution of your narrative. How adaptable is your brand story in response to the changing dynamics, needs or sentiments of the community? Are you continuously refining and evolving your narrative so it remains relevant and compelling?

The depth and richness of your narrative are so important. How are you utilizing various storytelling mediums – be it through content, visuals or experiences – to convey your brand story effectively? How can you leverage these mediums to captivate people further?

CHAPTER 3

Building Your Tribe: Strategies for Attracting and Engaging Community

There's a well-known quote from Amy Lee: 'Your vibe attracts your tribe.' The energy you put out draws like-minded people towards you, forming your community. So how do you create a positive vibe to attract a group of people who share your values and passions?

Communities are more than just gatherings of similar individuals; they're ecosystems where ideas flourish. They're spaces where people can find resonance and connection. At the core of every thriving community is a sense of belonging, and cultivating this is an art that involves empathy, trust and authenticity.

The strategic significance of building a 'tribe' in today's competitive landscape should not be overlooked, and it's imperative you understand that your audience isn't just a demographic, it is a collective of individuals with unique expertise, aspirations and challenges. Once you clearly understand this, you will know how to attract and engage with them.

Since their launch in 2017, the UK Black Business Show and UK Black Business Week have experienced remarkable growth. Initially, I began by posting daily inspirational quotes on Instagram, aiming to build a following through consistent engagement. The strategy was simple yet effective: by sharing positive and motivational messages tailored to Black professionals and entrepreneurs, I hoped to encourage widespread sharing and, in turn, attract more followers to the page. This approach was driven by a clear purpose – to cultivate a community, or tribe, of like-minded people who aligned with the values and aspirations highlighted in the quotes I was sharing.

That simple yet strategic approach showcases the power of consistent engagement and targeted content when it comes to community-building. It also highlights the importance of clarity in purpose when building your tribe.

Rebekah Taitt leads the Midlands Regional Development programme within the Business and Commercial Banking division of Lloyds. Her role involves building meaningful relationships and collaborating with business leaders and enterprises in Birmingham, as well as various local political and non-political figures.

She spoke to me about the challenges of building a tribe: 'It's really difficult. I have done it and it went wrong, where I was trying to embrace everyone, and I have done it and it's gone well – being very specific and targeted. Your tribe needs to have a shared sense of attitudes or characteristics. It's the first part, "attitudes", which I think is the most important and can shape the success of an authentic vibe in your tribe.'

Rebekah advocates for a deliberate approach to defining what her tribe stands for and actively seeking out members who align with those core attitudes. This strategy not only ensures a coherent community identity, but also ensures that engagement is meaningful and self-sustaining. Members are more likely to participate, contribute and advocate for a community that reflects their own attitudes and values, leading to a more dynamic and interactive group. A key takeaway is the importance of identifying and emphasizing shared attitudes as a foundational strategy for attracting and engaging with a community, ensuring that the group's vibe remains authentic for its members.

Cecil Peters also touched on this when he discussed how some people even joined his company because of the personal brand he had built. He told me, 'If you set out to create a positive and authentic culture without an understanding of and empathy for those that start from a place of disadvantage, then it may not achieve the aims you desire.' His approach is 'to be a positive and authentic person, rather than try to manipulate the environment. I have found that like-minded individuals are attracted by the potential of being in a positive conversation, with all the aspiration it creates. Within my company, people have told me that they joined the firm because they know my brand and wanted to work where I work. They felt it was a company where if I can be myself, they too can be themselves.'

A genuine approach, where leaders embody the values of positivity and authenticity, serves as a powerful magnet for like-minded individuals. This highlights the importance of personal examples over attempts to engineer a community's culture artificially. By focusing on being a positive and authentic figure, Cecil naturally attracted those who connected with his values.

Individual leaders' brands play a powerful role in shaping perceptions of the workplace. When leaders are perceived as authentic and positive, it signals to potential community members or employees that the organization values these traits, creating an environment where individuals feel encouraged to express themselves fully and engage more deeply with their work and community.

Cecil led by example in promoting a positive and authentic culture, and created a ripple effect, setting a standard for interactions and engagement within the organization. When leaders prioritize authenticity and positivity in their actions and interactions, they lay the foundation for an energized, engaged community where members feel valued, understood and inspired to be their best selves. This approach not only enhances the attractiveness of the community or organization but also ensures its long-term vibrancy and cohesion.

Chris Skeith also broke down what he believes are the traits of having an authentic vibe. Chris is the chief executive officer of the Association of Event Organisers (AEO), the leading association in its field in the UK. In the Queen's Birthday Honours list of 2021, he was awarded an OBE for services to the events industry. He told me, 'There are numerous commentators and theories on how to cultivate an authentic vibe, yet, for me, authenticity revolves around genuine practices – listening, honesty, fulfilling promises and transparent communication. In my journey, these principles have proven successful and enable followership and engagement.

'Leading an association with a diverse community with many common, but often specific, needs requires me to harmonize objectives and gain agreement to overall tactics. The key is to set up for success rather than failure. Ensuring that everyone's perspective is heard and integrating community and team input to create overarching objectives is crucial. Communicating the plan transparently and consistently, followed by effective implementation and updates, forms the cornerstone. Though not rocket science, it is paramount not to overlook these fundamentals.'

When you build your tribe or community, you're effectively taking the extra step to make sure they have room to address their needs in the way that suits them best; when you engage with them, their insights can help you improve your internal processes to ensure you are serving your community effectively. Allowing space for your community to express their thoughts can prompt them to invite new members through referrals and word-of-mouth marketing.

Reflecting on the genesis of the UK Black Business Show, it became evident that attracting a specific audience was crucial, yet the methodology for doing so remained elusive. And once the audience was attracted, the next challenge for me was how to engage effectively with them.

Attracting people to a community is like finding talent, and engaging them means keeping them interested. If you don't engage with them effectively, you might lose those you worked so hard to bring in, making all your initial efforts go to waste. Attraction and engagement are equally important. Companies should focus as much on keeping the right talent as they do on bringing it in.

This notion of the 'right talent' acknowledges that not everyone drawn to a community or a company aligns with its ethos, necessitating a deliberate disengagement at times. Crucially, the way engagement is approached can significantly influence the perception and dialogue surrounding a community or company. So, how do you navigate the delicate balance of attracting the right individuals and providing engaging experiences to retain them within your community or organization?

As Lynsey Campbell told me, 'It's about ensuring the community you are creating has a strong identity and purpose that is clear in all social communications and events, and that this identity is clear in all outward actions and communications. Those that join are always going to be the "right" people, as a by-product of the clear vision and purpose. Keeping communities engaged? It's all about delegation of authority in the right places, giving everyone a voice, being democratic in your approach, and knowing where to amplify and grow skills and voices in your community.'

This insight emphasizes the foundational step of defining and communicating core values and objectives across all platforms and interactions. When a community's vision and purpose are articulated clearly and consistently, this will naturally attract individuals who align with these principles, effectively self-selecting the 'right' members, whose values and interests reverberate with the community's ethos.

Once these individuals are attracted to the community, the focus then shifts to engagement and retention, which require a proactive and inclusive approach. Delegating and giving others a voice are crucial steps in creating a sense of ownership among community members. This democratic approach ensures that members feel valued and heard, increasing their commitment to and participation in the community.

Indie Gordon also talked about the challenges of building a tribe and how she overcame them. 'Building these incredible communities, we sometimes end up boxing ourselves into this idea that we're all the same just because we share a few common traits like skin colour, heritage or gender. But reality check: even within an under-represented group, there are layers of privilege that shape how we experience things. I've felt this on a personal level, realizing that people's approaches to achieving things can be quite different based on the privileges they've had.

'So the challenge is that it's like walking a tightrope, finding that sweet spot between being super inclusive and still keeping our community vibes intact. I'm all about embracing diverse perspectives and interests, yet I don't want us to lose sight of who we are and what we stand for. It's this delicate balance, this tension we navigate, making room for everyone while holding on to the core identity that brought us together in the first place, and as we grow this has often become a point of challenge that we have to work through – and let's be real, it's not always a walk in the park.

'There are these moments of figuring out how to blend inclusivity with maintaining a clear community identity. But you know what? It's in these challenges that we, as a community, truly learn, grow and build something special. It's about finding that balance, recognizing differences, and celebrating them, all while staying true to the heart of our community. We're all on this ongoing journey together.

'When it comes to tackling these challenges, I've found that open and transparent communication within the community is key. I want members to share their experiences, perspectives and expectations openly because it's incredible if this community is where you think you belong! But if not, a community out there is just right for you. You're never alone in this. For me, it's not about a one-size-fits-all solution. It's about creating an ongoing dialogue, adapting strategies, and enjoying the shared journey of learning, growing and celebrating the unique ecosystem that makes our community truly special.'

There are many complexities and nuances to consider when building and sustaining a community, especially one rooted in shared characteristics such as skin colour, heritage or gender. There is a diversity of experiences even within underrepresented groups, and it is important to recognize and navigate the layers of privilege that can influence people's perspectives and experiences. This challenges the notion of homogeneity, emphasizing that shared traits do not equate to uniformity in experiences or viewpoints.

As Indie describes it, maintaining inclusivity while preserving the unique identity and core values that define a community is a tightrope walk. This balance is crucial in order to create a space that welcomes diverse perspectives and experiences without diluting the foundational principles that unite its members. The tension between broadening inclusivity and maintaining a clear community identity is both a challenge and an opportunity for growth and learning.

Indie advocates for a flexible, dialogue-driven approach to community-building that values diversity and inclusivity as strengths. A vibrant community should embrace differences, celebrate individuality and evolve continuously, while also staying anchored to its core values. By keeping the conversation going and adapting strategies based on member feedback, communities can navigate the complexities of inclusivity and identity, crafting a shared journey that is both enriching and unifying.

Building a community is like planning an exciting journey where individuals don't just spectate but actively participate. So, as we navigate how to build a tribe and strategies for engaging a community, let's pause and ask ourselves how we can ensure active participation. How do we turn passive observers into passionate advocates? How do we create a space where voices resonate and souls connect?

Finding Your Target Audience and Understanding Their Needs

Nothing holds as much weight as truly understanding and connecting with your target audience. Identifying this core demographic isn't just about creating a superficial profile; it's about delving into their needs, desires, aspirations and pain points.

Imagine trying to build a house without a blueprint. Similarly, attempting to create a community without a deep understanding of who it's meant for can lead to instability and confusion. Only through truly immersing yourself in the world of your community's members can you truly craft a space that becomes a sanctuary – one that caters to their requirements, tackles their pain points and provides bona fide solutions.

Andy Ayim MBE told me about how understanding his audience led to significant breakthroughs in his endeavours. 'Working with start-ups and venture capitalists provided me insight into the lack of funding going to Black founders in the UK. Black founders in the United Kingdom raised only 0.95 per cent of all venture investment allocated in the country so far this year (or just $165 million out of around $17.3 billion), according to a report by Extend Ventures.

'Therefore, this awareness of the lack of capital and access to networks birthed a new community project in 2023 called the 678 Club. A private community of Black founders that generate six figures or more in annual revenue. Once a quarter we run tactical seminars for this network to form meaningful relationships and learn best-in-class industry lessons to enable them to scale their ambition and grow their businesses.

'A great example of our community events was in July 2023. We ran a seminar titled "Planning for an Exit" where I interviewed a successful Black founder who sold his social marketing agency for an undisclosed sum. These sessions create a safe space to knowledge-share and pass on information that traditionally is difficult to come by and access.'

The creation of the 678 Club in response to the stark underfunding of Black founders in the UK is a targeted approach to community-building, one that not only acknowledges a gap in the ecosystem but actively seeks to bridge it. By focusing on Black founders generating significant annual revenue, Andy is directly addressing the challenges of capital access and network limitations, offering a specialized platform for growth and support.

Community events such as the seminar are not just gatherings; they are designed to fulfil the specific informational and networking needs of the community. By offering a safe space for knowledge-sharing on topics that are critically relevant yet traditionally inaccessible to Black founders, the 678 Club leverages its understanding of its audience to create meaningful engagement and provide tangible value to its members.

Such targeted strategies lead to significant breakthroughs in community engagement, by ensuring that the content, opportunities and interactions provided are highly relevant and impactful. This not only helps attract members who are directly aligned with the community's purpose, but also encourages active participation and loyalty, as members recognize the unique benefits and support they receive.

Understanding the specific challenges, needs and aspirations of your audience allows for the creation of focused initiatives that offer substantial value and support. This in turn cultivates a highly engaged and committed community, capable of driving significant breakthroughs and achieving shared goals.

Jamelia Donaldson also emphasized the importance of understanding her audience's needs: 'Understanding our target audience has been vital to the success and evolution of TreasureTress. A significant breakthrough emerged from our commitment to deeply comprehending our customers' desires, leading to the establishment of our renowned pop-up experiences.

'The inspiration for these high-quality events originated from valuable customer feedback. Customers expressed two desires: 1) the wish to design their own box, and 2) an eagerness to receive product advice face to face.

'Taking heed of this insightful feedback, we embraced the challenge and just executed our sixth pop-up experience. Each iteration has seen us grow and surpass previous successes, continuously refining and expanding our offerings. This intimate understanding of our audience's preferences and needs not only enhanced customer satisfaction but also propelled TreasureTress to new heights as we consistently strive to deliver experiences that exceed expectations.'

This is an exemplary model of audience-centric strategy in action. By listening to and genuinely understanding their target audience's feedback, TreasureTress was able to innovate and introduce experiences that directly addressed two customer needs: personalized product selection and face-to-face interactions for product advice. The continued success of the pop-up experiences highlights the importance of not just the initial understanding of an audience but also ongoing engagement and adaptation to feedback. Each iteration of the event, informed by customer input, allowed TreasureTress to refine and expand their offerings, demonstrating a commitment to evolving in tandem with their audience's expectations. This approach has ensured a deeper connection with their community, and also serves as a differentiator in a competitive market, enhancing customer loyalty and satisfaction.

Leveraging direct customer feedback to inform service offerings exemplifies how understanding your audience can lead to significant breakthroughs. The most impactful innovations often stem from a deep, empathetic understanding of the community you serve. By prioritizing the desires and needs of their audience, TreasureTress not only enhanced their brand reputation but also created a more engaging and satisfying experience for their customers.

Robust communities can emerge from the individuals who are part of the intended audience. The UK Black Business Show stemmed from a place of discontent: the absence of gatherings catering to Black professionals and entrepreneurs. As a member of this community seeking such a platform, I endeavoured to establish a space grounded in my own experience, believing it would resonate with many others. The closer you are to your community, the stronger the connections will be.

Understanding your audience is a twofold endeavour. It's not just about comprehending who they are now but also forecasting where they're heading. Communities thrive on evolution and adaptation. By anticipating the changing needs and preferences of your audience, you're not just building for the present, you're crafting a resilient foundation that can weather the storms of change, ensuring longevity and relevance.

Frequently, the discourse revolves around financial fore-casting, yet the ability to anticipate the future needs and aspirations of your community will distinguish you from others. It's not just about predicting numbers; it's about foreseeing and addressing the evolving expectations and desires of those you serve.

Beyond the quantitative aspects, there's an emotional res-onance that comes with truly understanding your audience. It's about empathy – the ability to step into their shoes, to feel what they feel and understand their experiences. This empathy forms a foundation of trust, enabling connections to be forged that are not easily shaken. When community members feel seen, heard and understood, they become not just participants but passionate advocates, driving the community's growth through their unwavering support and dedication.

The importance of finding your target audience and truly understanding their needs cannot be exaggerated in the realm of community-building. It's about peeling back the layers, digging deep into the core of who your com-munity is, and moulding an environment that supports and enriches their lives. Only then can a community truly flourish and thrive.

How to Find Your Audience

Finding your audience can initially seem a daunting prospect. In the era of social media, the pressure to amass followers rapidly can be overwhelming. Countless stories of individuals swiftly building massive followings creates the illusion of ease. However, I challenge you to shift your focus away from mere numbers and instead concentrate on cultivating a *genuine* community. Having 10,000 followers with just a handful who genuinely care about your message is ultimately futile.

Early in my entrepreneurial journey, I made a conscious decision not to rely on friends' obligatory support. I didn't want them to follow me or come to my events unless they were truly interested. I wanted to attract people who were really into what I was doing, rather than just having friends and family around out of a sense of duty. While it's great to have their support, they alone won't make your community thrive.

If you're grappling with why your friends aren't engaging, perhaps your community doesn't align with their interests. Instead of fixating on their support, direct your attention to the multitude of individuals who *are* seeking the community you've created. Focus on identifying and connecting with those who genuinely identify with your message and vision.

Discovering your audience is the benchmark of community-building; comprehending where your community resides is of the utmost importance. Communities consist of individuals, and just as people evolve, so do communities. Their needs might change in the future. Grasping the nuances of your community's current demographic and anticipating their future requirements enables you to serve them effectively.

To identify your audience, there are several strategies at your disposal.

Conduct Comprehensive Market Research

Doing market research means you're finding out what people like and want. It helps businesses figure out exactly who they should be talking to, by asking people for their thoughts on different products or services. Although it might seem like a lot of work, it's an important step in getting to know your audience. Even if you think you know a lot, market research can surprise you with new information.

My first step when planning any event always involves comprehensive market research to gain a panoramic view of the market. Are there existing ventures similar to mine? How well do they fare? Where does my audience predominantly reside – on social platforms, at in-person gatherings, or both? Assessing the scale of an audience, their financial capacity, discerning whether it's a burgeoning community or they're just following a passing trend – these are among the multitude of crucial considerations integral to market exploration.

Consider market research as the guiding compass for your journey to cultivating a community. Plunge into demographic specifics, psychographic attributes and behavioural trends. Employ an array of tools – from surveys to interviews to data analytics – to extract deep insights.

Beyond merely identifying who they are, delve into the 'why' behind their desires or actions. Embrace both qualitative and quantitative methodologies, aiming not just for superficial data but identifying the underlying motivations steering their choices, preferences and challenges.

79

Demographic Analysis

Getting to know your audience starts with understanding basic information. Categories like age, gender, location, income and education level give you a rough idea of who they are. But the real trick is to dig deeper into these categories. Even within a certain age group, people can be really different in what they like and how they act. Within a specific age bracket, nuances in preferences and behaviours might significantly vary, shaping distinct pockets of interests and needs.

For instance, within the broader age range of 25–35, there might exist subsets with contrasting preferences – some might prioritize sustainability in product choices, while others might value affordability over eco-friendliness. Similarly, within a certain geographical location, micro-communities could emerge, each with its own cultural nuances and consumer habits. Recognizing these intricate variations illuminates the diverse landscape within demographics, allowing for a more nuanced approach to community-building.

However, demographics don't provide the complete narrative. They are a starting point – a framework to help you understand the surface characteristics of your audience. To truly create meaningful connections with your community, delving into psychographics and behavioural patterns is necessary. This digs deeper than just knowing who your audience is. It's about understanding why they do what they do, and how they make their choices.

Psychographics examine people's values, beliefs, interests and lifestyle choices. Unravelling these layers will allow you to understand your audience's motivations and aspirations, guiding the development of content and engagement strategies that will deeply resonate with them. The analysis of behavioural patterns, on the other hand, uncovers the actions and habits of your audience – what platforms they visit, how they consume content, and their purchasing behaviours.

Starting with basic information like age and location is just the beginning. To really know who your audience is, you need to look into their interests, values and why they do what they do. Getting the full picture helps you not only to find your audience, but also to build real relationships and lasting connections. By doing this, you will create a community that sticks around and stays active.

Psychographic Insights

It's all in the mind! Once you've looked at the statistics, it's crucial to understand what makes your audience tick. This means figuring out their values, what they're into, how they live their lives and what they believe in. These elements are the key to understanding the 'why' behind people's actions, revealing their motivations, aspirations and obstacles.

Recognizing that a specific segment of your audience prioritizes sustainability over price or experiences over possessions can significantly influence how you design your community and shape the offerings you provide. This goes beyond knowing who your audience is on paper; it's about understanding them on a fundamental level.

Psychographics reveal the hidden reasons and feelings that guide why people make certain choices: not just what your audience does, but why they do it. For instance, knowing that a subset of your audience values personal growth and continuous learning in particular might prompt you to offer educational resources or host events that cater specifically to their thirst for knowledge.

Understanding your audience's psychographics helps you to connect with them. It lets you create messages, content and experiences that match what they deeply care about and feel. This leads to an attachment and connection within your community that extends beyond surface-level engagement.

Behavioural Patterns

Even with careful planning, audience engagement can swiftly reveal a disconnection between what's offered and what they truly desire. This is where behavioural patterns emerge as the guiding light. Analysing these patterns leads to a deep understanding of how your audience interacts with content, products or services. It entails studying the intricacies of online behaviour, dissecting purchasing patterns, scrutinizing content-consumption habits, and ultimately creating engagement strategies that align seamlessly with their preferences.

For example, imagine you've put a lot of effort into creating content or a service that you think perfectly meets your audience's needs, but then it doesn't get much attention. This situation isn't necessarily a failure, but a chance to look into the data on how your audience behaves. It's like solving a puzzle where every action they take gives you a clue about what they really like and need. By understanding these subtle hints, you're not just reacting to what they say they want; you're getting ahead of what they haven't even mentioned. This helps you create a stronger and more intuitive connection with your community by really tuning in to their preferences.

Surveys and Interviews

Directly engaging with your potential audience through surveys and interviews unveils a treasure trove of insights. Crafting meticulously designed questions that probe into the depths of their motivations, aspirations and desires is an art form. Using these kinds of questions will help you understand things about your audience that simple numbers and stats might miss. They provide a platform for your audience to express themselves, allowing their voices to paint a vivid picture of their needs, desires and challenges.

Imagine the insight gained from listening first-hand to your audience's narratives – the context behind their choices, the emotional triggers guiding their decisions. These qualitative approaches are more than just data-collection exercises; they create a genuine connection between you and your audience. They enable you to step into their shoes, empathize with their experiences, and gain insights that are vital in crafting solutions and offerings that genuinely resonate. This direct line of communication not only amplifies their voices but also ensures that your community-building endeavours are rooted in a deep understanding of the human stories and sentiments behind the numbers and statistics.

Data Analysis Tools

Use tools that analyse data to learn more from the information you already have. These tools can help you understand how people feel about things, spot trends, and group your audience into different categories. By looking closely at the data, you can find patterns and connections that aren't obvious right away. This lets you make smarter choices based on solid facts.

Competitor Analysis

Frequently, when discussing competitors with people, I encounter a spectrum of responses. Some demonstrate a keen awareness of the competitive landscape, while others appear somewhat deluded, asserting that they have no direct competitors. While there might be rare instances where this holds true for specific companies, even the most significant and successful companies operate within competitive spheres. The claim that you have no competitors is not a credible one.

However, acknowledging competitors doesn't mean being consumed by them. There's immense value in studying competitors without falling into the trap of imitation. Understanding their strategies, dissecting their strengths and weaknesses, and observing their audience engagement tactics can offer a wealth of knowledge. This analytical approach not only unveils potential gaps or opportunities in the market, but also serves as a benchmark against which you can evaluate and elevate your own community-building strategies.

Market analysis combines numbers and other detailed information to give you a full picture of the people you want to reach. It goes beyond merely identifying competitors; it amalgamates quantitative and qualitative data through diverse methodologies, creating a comprehensive understanding of your target audience. It's also not just about knowing who your audience is, but rather unravelling the particulars of why they make certain choices and behave in particular ways. Armed with this information, you can address their needs, aspirations and challenges with precision and effectiveness.

Engaging in Active Social Listening

'The art of conversation lies in listening' is a quote from Malcom Forbes. Listening isn't just a precursor to speaking; it's what enables meaningful dialogue. How can you truly engage with or speak to a community without first hearing what they're saying? The dynamics of communication lie at the heart of attracting and engaging with your audience.

'Social listening' is a crucial strategy that involves paying close attention to what people are saying about your brand, your competitors and your industry as a whole. When you get involved in these discussions, invaluable insights will surface, and these will be essential in informing your decisions about your community's growth and direction.

The online world has a lot of valuable information waiting to be found. Social listening helps you keep an eye on what people are talking about, how they feel, and what new things are becoming popular on different websites and apps. The real key isn't to just watch what people are saying, but to really understand the trends and topics that matter in your area or industry. By actively listening – absorbing their language, understanding their interests and empathizing with their concerns – you get unfiltered glimpses into your audience's thoughts, desires and pain points. These unvarnished insights will then help you craft content and initiatives that authentically and significantly impact your community.

Social Listening Tools

There are a few online tools designed for social listening; these tools allow you to monitor mentions, keywords and hashtags related to your niche across various social media platforms. Platforms like Hootsuite, Sprout Social and Brandwatch contain features that track brand mentions, sentiment analysis and audience demographics. These tools help in gathering real-time data about discussions, trends and sentiments among your target audience.

Monitoring Conversations and Trends

Attentiveness is not just a trait; it's a strategic advantage. Keeping a close eye on what's happening online and what matters to your audience – in groups, forums, blogs or on social media – is how you win. The wealth of insight gained from this is invaluable. As you immerse yourself in your community's ethos, your understanding becomes stronger, affording you the ability to align authentically with their evolving interests and concerns. An acute understanding of your audience serves as a compass guiding your engagement, ensuring that every initiative and communication is threaded with relevance and authenticity.

Identifying Pain Points and Need

Social listening is a powerful tool in unearthing the pain points, challenges and unmet needs articulated by your audience. By dissecting the complaints, queries or suggestions that populate discussions, you will identify areas where your community can extend support, provide solutions or curate invaluable content. This offers a blueprint for fortifying your community as an indispensable resource – one that not only acknowledges but actively addresses real, tangible needs.

Understanding these pain points isn't just about identifying areas for improvement; it's about strategically positioning your community as an empathetic and proactive ally, able to cater to the authentic requirements of your audience. This transformation from a passive listener to an active problem-solver ensures that your community will become an indispensable asset.

Tracking Sentiments and Emotions

Monitoring the pulse of your audience goes beyond mere words – it encompasses the emotional undertones. Social listening tools that are equipped with sentiment analysis decode not just what's said but how it's expressed. This grasp of emotional context helps with the creation of content and strategies that intimately connect with your audience's emotions and lived experiences.

Engaging in Direct Conversation

Active engagement with your audience – be it through discussions, addressing feedback or answering queries – serves as more than just a community-building exercise; it's an invaluable conduit through which to gain first-hand insight into their thoughts, nuanced preferences and pressing pain points. This hands-on approach humanizes your brand or community, creating an environment of trust and connection. These interactions create authenticity, allowing your audience to see the heart and soul behind the brand and establishing a genuine rapport.

Adapting Content and Strategies

Harnessing insights from social listening isn't just about passive observation; it's about refining your content approach and community endeavours. By discerning the pulse of your audience, you can pivot and mould your content strategy to encompass their interests and needs. Furthermore, tailoring your engagement strategies to align with their preferred platforms and communication styles is essential for meaningful interaction.

I spoke with Antoinette and Tayo Oguntonade about adapting content based on listening to the community. Antoinette and Tayo founded BrickzWithTipz in 2019, from a shared desire to provide a welcoming space for individuals to unravel the complexities of property and finance in a relatable manner. Since its inception, BrickzWithTipz has leveraged Antoinette and Tayo's industry expertise and professional qualifications in order to engage with an audience exceeding 100,000 across various social media platforms.

They explained: 'Building a business from scratch can sometimes lead us to believe we always know what our community needs, but these needs can change over time. For instance, by listening to our audience, we've learned that the optimal time for webinars is 7 p.m., and initially we understood that people, often pressed for time, preferred these not to exceed an hour. However, through running polls and continuously gathering feedback, we discovered that this preference is topic-dependent. A key insight was that people are willing to dedicate more time to topics they find especially important.'

Active social listening isn't just eavesdropping on digital conversations; it's deciphering the unspoken sentiments, below-the-surface emotions and unmet needs. These insights then lay a foundation upon which to craft content, initiatives and engagement strategies that authentically bridge the gap between your community and your brand.

Creating Persona Profiles and Empathy Maps

Persona profiles and empathy maps infuse life into quantitative data. To construct comprehensive persona profiles representing your envisioned community, you must investigate their daily routines, motivations, hurdles and aspirations. These detailed portraits serve as windows into their lives, illuminating the minutiae that define their journey. Empathy maps further enrich this understanding by offering a visual representation of their experiences, thoughts, emotions and actions across various touchpoints. Empathy maps typically include sections such as 'What they think and feel', 'What they see', 'What they say and do', and 'Pains and gains'. This visualization aids in understanding the emotional landscape of your audience, allowing you to empathize with their experiences.

Stepping into their world enables you to comprehend their needs, laying the groundwork for shaping your community in ways that authentically cater to and fulfil those needs. It's about not just knowing who they are, but also intimately understanding what drives them, and ensuring that your community becomes a nurturing space that resonates with their deepest aspirations and desires.

Creating persona profiles is like making up characters for a story. These characters represent different kinds of people in your community, showing their unique likes, wants and challenges. To make these characters, you gather information from different places: looking at market trends, seeing what people say online and talking to people directly. Then, you mix all this information together to show what these people might do, dream about and face in their lives. Instead of just looking at numbers and charts, you give these characters names, stories and backgrounds, making them feel like real people. This way, when you think about your audience, you're not just seeing data; you're understanding real human stories and what drives different people. This helps foster a stronger connection and understanding of who you're reaching out to.

For example, when we were creating the Soar membership platform for entrepreneurs, we discussed a character named 'Shelley', a working mum in her thirties with a side hustle who does not have time to attend networking events or consume educational content. We learned about Shelley's needs and challenges by researching and talking to real people like her. Then we thought about how our membership platform could fit into her life – maybe by offering a WhatsApp group for networking, or online workshops and webinars she could watch on her lunch break. By thinking about Shelley's story, we made our membership more useful and appealing to real people facing similar situations.

How to Develop a Persona Profile

I. MOTIVATIONS AND GOALS

To create an accurate persona profile, you'll need to understand their motivations, goals and aspirations. Understand what drives them, what they seek to achieve, and the challenges they face. Some personas might prioritize physical interactions and others might value social media interactions more. Knowing these nuances will help tailor your community offerings to cater to diverse needs effectively.

2. PAIN POINTS AND CHALLENGES

Each persona will have their own pain points, challenges and frustrations. You need to understand the obstacles, fears and barriers that hinder their specific journey. Recognizing these pain points helps in developing solutions or support mechanisms within your community to address these needs.

3. AUDIENCE SEGMENTS

Personas serve as a humanized representation of audience insights. They help in internalizing data and transforming it into relatable stories and scenarios. By personifying segments of your audience, you and your team can better empathize with and understand the diverse needs and motivations of your community members.

*

Persona profiles and empathy maps are compasses that guide community design, content curation and engagement tactics. They help to shape messaging, initiatives and services, ensuring they resonate with personas that represent a potential or existing audience. Whether it involves refining user interfaces for seamless interaction or sculpting content to address core struggles, these tools help you to align your content and delivery meticulously with your audience's needs.

Ultimately, crafting persona profiles and empathy maps breathes life into raw audience data, unlocking new insights into the multifaceted motivations, obstacles and aspirations of community members.

Engaging in Community Groups and Forums

Consider your community niche, and proactively engage in online forums, groups and other communities that orbit around this niche. Immersing yourself in these spheres grants first-hand exposure to your audience's intricacies – their interests, challenges and preferences. While navigating these spaces, maintain a watchful eye. Within these groups lie potential influencers and thought leaders whose impact could significantly aid in propelling your community's growth. Cultivating relationships within these spaces not only fosters connections but also provides invaluable insights on your voyage towards cultivating a robust and interconnected community.

These engagements are not just opportunities for networking; they're gateways to understanding your audience, revealing layers that statistical data alone might not reveal and ultimately helping you on your community-building journey.

Relevant Communities

Positioning yourself strategically requires pinpointing the arenas that harmonize with your community's essence. Start by identifying online/offline platforms – be it X (formerly known as Twitter), Reddit, Facebook, meet-ups, Instagram pages, LinkedIn groups or specialized forums – that relate to your community's niche. The litmus test for relevance lies within the personas you've meticulously crafted: do these groups or platforms resonate with their qualities and attributes? If these platforms mirror the characteristics of your identified personas, then they can serve as hubs that demand your active participation and presence.

Identifying the online forums, social media communities and discussion spaces that sync harmoniously with your community's identity is just the beginning. Delve deeper, beyond the surface-level alignment, and seek the nuances that truly resonate with your audience's aspirations, challenges and preferences. These platforms and spaces aren't mere gathering spots; they're the portals through which you will decode your community's needs and desires, forging connections and gathering insights that help you facilitate your audience's collective journey.

Actively Participate and Observe

Engaging actively once you've located these spaces is more than just observation; contribute, share valuable insights and partake in ongoing conversations. This active participation isn't about showcasing your presence; it's to allow you to absorb the essence of the community's culture firsthand. By plunging into these discussions, you navigate real-time nuanced interactions, deciphering not just what is said but also how it's communicated. This hands-on approach will uncover a treasure trove of crucial information.

Take Notes and Learn

In these spaces, the immediate instinct might be to launch into promotion mode for your community or one you wish to build. However, the real power lies in the art of listening before promoting. Resist the urge to broadcast; instead, focus on actively hearing what others are saying.

Direct your attention towards deciphering the conversations unfolding among those in this space. Dive deep into understanding their lexicon, the challenges they grapple with and the solutions they fervently seek. This observant approach isn't just surface-level; it reveals intricate layers of insight into your potential audience – the genuine interests, nuanced preferences and pain points that drive their interactions. Embracing this attentive stance sets the stage for crafting strategies and offerings that meet your community's needs and aspirations.

Build Relationships and Trust

Establishing meaningful relationships within these communities holds profound significance; authenticity in engagement is pivotal. These connections are avenues for fostering genuine bonds with members and influencers alike. Instead of focusing solely on what you aim to gain, contemplate what you can contribute to a space. Offer value generously – whether it's sharing expertise, proffering solutions, or engaging in substantive conversations that enrich the discourse. Nurturing these connections isn't just about fostering trust; it's about cultivating a reputation as a credible and knowledgeable participant who contributes meaningfully to a community's growth and evolution.

Identify Influencers and Thought Leaders

As you cultivate relationships and foster trust, this will lead to a buy-in from your community. Channel your focus towards identifying influential figures and thought leaders who have considerable sway in terms of steering the community's conversations and trajectory. Forming bonds with these influencers goes beyond networking; it's an avenue to expand your reach and enhance your credibility. These influential figures possess the potential to amplify your voice and impact when the time comes to unveil and nurture your own community. Embracing these relationships isn't just about establishing connections; it's about aligning with influential voices capable of galvanizing support and driving the communal momentum towards your shared vision.

Respect Community Guidelines

When you make yourself part of established groups or communities, it's really important to follow their rules and respect their values and moral principles. This isn't just about doing what you're told; it's about truly respecting what these communities stand for. When you're interacting within these groups, make sure you're not just there to promote yourself. Instead, focus on being helpful and creating real connections with people. If you value mutual respect and giving back, this will help build trust and lasting relationships.

Gold Mines for Community Design

The raw gems of information gained from engaging in community groups and forums should not merely be noted but cherished. Use what you learn to shape your community – deciding how it looks, what you talk about and how you connect with people. Pay close attention to what people in these groups need, what they want, and what problems they encounter, and use this important information to help you.

Established online forums and groups offer a front-row seat to a dynamic community. Joining them is an opportunity to plunge into an audience's sphere, fostering connections and harvesting invaluable insights to help you in your community-building endeavours. These spaces are gold mines, offering a wealth of data that can guide the trajectory of your strategies, content creation and engagement methodologies for the community you aim to cultivate.

Experiment, Iterate and Analyse

Achieving perfection from the outset is an elusive pursuit; embracing failure and learning from missteps is a crucial aspect of community-building. Grant yourself the freedom to stumble along the way. Consider launching pilot initiatives, smaller-scale versions or experimental campaigns within your community framework. Scrutinize engagement metrics, ardently seek feedback and meticulously analyse outcomes, and hone and refine your approach based on real-time feedback. This journey of experimentation isn't just about trial and error; it's a means to test hypotheses and validate assumptions. Each iteration not only deepens your understanding of your audience, it also facilitates the fine-tuning of your offerings, aligning them more closely with your community's evolving needs and preferences.

Discovering your audience is a multifaceted endeavour that involves a combination of data analysis, active listening, empathetic understanding, immersion in existing communities and iterative refinement. Each of these methods reveals an aspect of your audience; the journey to finding your audience isn't static – it's a dynamic process of exploration, discovery and adaptation, ensuring you and your work remain relevant and impactful.

Pilot Initiatives

Smaller-scale initiatives can be useful as experiments – to test novel ideas, diverse engagement strategies or innovative content formats. Whether it's inaugurating a webinar series, initiating vibrant discussions, or unveiling new features of a product, these ventures offer invaluable insights without you committing fully to a comprehensive implementation. This approach not only conserves resources but also serves as a litmus test – allowing you to gauge the pulse of your audience and the viability of the endeavour on a larger scale.

Reflecting on the UK Black Business Show's inception, initially booking a venue for 250 attendees instead of diving headfirst into a huge event proved instrumental. This cautious approach didn't limit potential, but rather demonstrated a real appetite within the community for such a gathering. This approach not only minimized risk but also spotlighted a tangible audience, leading to a burgeoning waiting list of individuals eager to attend future events. It was a testament to the power of starting small to understand the true dimensions of a community's hunger and future participation.

Gather Real-Time Feedback

Encourage community members to provide feedback on these pilot initiatives. Utilize surveys, polls or direct feedback channels to gather insight on what worked well, what could be improved, and what aspects reverberated most with the audience. Actively listen to people's opinions and suggestions, as this will help you improve.

Analyse Engagement Metrics

Feedback is important, but you should also be tracking and analysing key engagement metrics related to pilot initiatives. Monitor metrics like participation rates, engagement levels, conversion rates and user behaviour patterns. Quantitative data provides objective insights into the success or shortcomings of your experiments.

Embrace Iteration and Improvement

Use the feedback and data collected to refine your approach. Identify areas that need improvement and areas that resonated positively with your audience. Adjust your strategies, content or features based on these findings. Iteration allows you to optimize and enhance your community offerings continually.

A/B Testing and Variations*

Experiment with variations or A/B testing to compare different approaches. Test different types of content,

---

* A/B testing, also known as split testing, refers to a randomized experimentation process wherein two or more versions of a variable (web page, page element, etc.) are shown to different segments of website visitors at the same time to determine which version leaves the maximum impact and drives business metrics.[9]

engagement tactics or community features to understand what generates better responses from your audience. This method helps in understanding preferences and optimizing strategies based on empirical data.

Measure Impact and ROI

Assess the impact of your experiments in terms of the Return on Investment (ROI). As well as quantitative metrics, also measure qualitative aspects like brand perception, member satisfaction and community sentiment to determine both the tangible and intangible benefits.

Scale Successful Strategies

Identify strategies or elements that yield positive results and scale them up within your community. Implement successful approaches on a larger scale while continuing to fine-tune them based on ongoing feedback and analysis.

The cycle of experimentation, iteration and analysis forms a continuous loop of improvement within your community-building endeavours, and ensures that your strategies are not static but evolve based on real-time data and community feedback. By embracing experimentation and adaptation, you will be able to scale successfully and also create a community that is responsive, innovative, and aligned with the evolving needs and preferences of your audience.

Creating compelling content

Community-building isn't just about establishing a presence; it's about orchestrating a symphony of captivating content and transformative experiences. Creating content that stands out and really connects with people in the noisy online world is an art.

It's important to learn what makes content and experiences interesting. There are secrets behind the stories that touch our hearts, and ways to get people involved. It's the small details that make experiences go beyond the surface and have a lasting effect on how we connect with each other.

Craft Authentic and Relevant Stories

Authenticity is the heartbeat of compelling content. Share stories that connect with your audience on a personal level. Whether it's through testimonials or behind-the-scenes glimpses or relatable narratives, humanize your content to evoke emotions and spark engagement. Additionally, ensure your content is relevant to the interests and context of your community.

Diversify Content Formats and Channels

Embrace diversity in content formats to cater to varied preferences. Experiment with different content types such as videos, blogs, podcasts, infographics, live streams and interactive content. Each format offers a unique way to engage with your audience. Moreover, leverage multiple channels where your community resides – social media, forums, newsletters and dedicated platforms. Tailor content distribution to reach your audience where they are most active, optimizing engagement across different platforms and mediums.

Variety is the spice of engaging content. Visual learners might prefer videos or infographics, while others might enjoy in-depth written content or podcasts for their commute. Consider the platforms and channels your community prefers to hear from you on. Tailor your content distribution to fit these platforms – create 'snackable' content for social media, thoughtful long-form content for your website or blog, and interactive sessions for live streams or webinars. Engaging your audience in the places where they are most active amplifies your content's impact.

There's no one-size-fits-all approach to creating compelling content. It's a continuous journey of learning, adapting and refining based on your audience's evolving needs and preferences. The art lies in striking a balance between resonating with your community's core values and being agile enough to innovate and experiment with new approaches. By understanding, empathizing and engaging with your audience, you can curate content that fosters genuine connections, sparks conversations and keeps people coming back for more.

CHAPTER 4

Creating a Thriving Community in Business

Business success isn't solely defined by profit margins and market dominance.

Whether you're an employee seeking personal fulfilment, an employer striving for an engaged workforce, or a business owner eyeing sustainable growth, the essence of community within the workplace is the way forward.

Collaboration is more than a corporate buzzword; it's the key to innovation and success, and community is at the centre of it all.

Several advantages sprout from developing a strong community within the workplace. From enhancing job satisfaction and productivity to creating an atmosphere of inclusivity and support, the benefits extend far beyond conventional corporate metrics. As we look at these facets in this chapter, we'll examine multiple strategies aimed at nurturing a positive work environment.

A strong community can also significantly elevate individual career trajectories, and having a supportive network in the workplace can pave the way for both professional advancement and personal development. It's important to understand the role that communities play in shaping your journey up the career ladder.

The Importance of Community in the Workplace

As the lines between work and life continue to blur, the concept of community in the workplace has taken on unprecedented importance.

The workplace has evolved beyond a mere location for earning a salary; it has become a significant part of our lives. Colleagues are more than just 'associates'. It's increasingly common to spend time with them outside of office hours, engaging in social activities like grabbing drinks or even inviting them to personal celebrations such as weddings and birthday parties. Thinking back to one of the most significant days of my life, my wedding day, both my wife and I had invited several people whom we had met along the way in our careers. After school and university, work is the most likely place for building new relationships and even potentially meeting your life partner. As we spend more time at work, whether that's virtually or in person, organizations need to invest time and effort into developing an environment where employees can grow, flourish and prosper.

Shelley Bishton is the Head of Diversity, Equity and Inclusion at News UK. In her role, Shelley focuses on furthering DEI strategy in multiple brands across the company. We spoke about the importance of community in the workplace. 'It is estimated that we will spend a third of our life or 90,000 hours working,' she said. 'Imagine working all those hours and not feeling a sense of community in those spaces, for all that time? But yet, we often feel like we can't be ourselves at work. We mask or hide elements of ourselves. We decide to hide parts of ourselves or downplay parts of ourselves in order to fit into the "corporate space". It wasn't until I found my confidence within myself that I began to own my own authentic vibe. My community helps me to continue walking in my truth, as by doing so, it lifts them too.'

By presenting herself as authentic and navigating corporate spaces with confidence, Shelley not only finds personal fulfilment but also encourages others to embrace their true selves.

Jamelia Donaldson also provided some insight on community-building in the workplace and what she has found effective. 'I often think about Gareth Southgate's press speech during a crucial moment in the World Cup. When Raheem Sterling had to rush home for a family emergency, Southgate emphasized, "There are more important things than football." I can identify with this approach. While we all care passionately about the work we do, it's crucial to recognize that the significance of our work cannot overshadow our duty of care for each other as human beings, our cultural community, and our commitment as colleagues united in a shared mission.'

Jamelia draws a powerful parallel between leadership in sports and effective community-building in the workplace, emphasizing the importance of empathy, understanding and shared humanity when creating a collaborative environment. Her Gareth Southgate example highlights a leadership approach that values individuals' well-being above professional achievements – key to creating a sense of community among colleagues. It is a poignant reminder of the power of empathetic leadership and the value of prioritizing human connections within the workplace.

Effective community-building in the workplace revolves around recognizing and addressing the multifaceted lives of employees, and acknowledging that while work is a significant part of life, it is not the whole story. Leaders who embrace this principle, as Southgate did, demonstrate a commitment to their team's holistic well-being, which in turn creates a culture of mutual support and understanding. This approach not only strengthens interpersonal relationships but also enhances team cohesion, as colleagues feel valued and supported not just for their professional contributions but as individuals with lives outside of work.

Adopting strategies like regular check-ins, open forums for sharing personal as well as professional challenges, and flexible policies that accommodate personal needs are all practical ways to integrate this philosophy into workplace culture. Celebrating non-work achievements and milestones builds a rapport and a sense of appreciation that goes beyond work-related interactions.

Having a 'duty of care' for each other reinforces the idea that the workplace community is a support network that rallies in times of need, echoing the sentiment that there are indeed 'more important things' than work. This does not diminish the passion or commitment to the shared mission, but rather enriches it by building a foundation of trust and mutual respect.

The process of workplace community-building is multi-faceted, from understanding the core principles that underpin a thriving community to implementing practical strategies that promote inclusivity and a sense of belonging.

Enhancing the Workplace Experience as a Professional

As a working professional, you have the power to enhance your workplace experience significantly by actively engaging in and contributing to your community. Don't just be a bystander, start to initiate and participate in activities that enhance camaraderie among your colleagues.

Reflecting on one of my first jobs, I remember a colleague who founded a running club at our workplace. His passion for running and fitness was evident, and he sought companionship in this journey towards well-being. By the year's end, he had successfully gathered a dedicated cohort of 15–20 individuals who joined him for runs between 6 and 7 a.m. before starting their workday. What truly stood out to me about his initiative was its dynamic nature; it wasn't always the same set of faces at these runs, but rather a diverse group from across the organization.

The running club did not only impact physical fitness. It facilitated unprecedented connections throughout the company, bridging gaps between senior and junior staff and creating a robust community that bonded over a shared interest in health and fitness. This endeavour didn't just create a group of runners; it created strong relationships among colleagues, enriching the workplace culture in a positive way.

As the running club gained momentum, my colleague began to host weekend marathons, charity runs and fitness challenges, further solidifying his presence within the company. Initially motivated by personal fitness goals, he became an inadvertent wellness ambassador, inspiring people to improve their physical well-being but also their mental and social health.

The running club's influence extended beyond its early members. Colleagues who had never considered themselves runners started to take interest, motivated by the visible improvements in health, mood and productivity seen in the running club members. The club also initiated a buddy system, pairing seasoned runners with beginners to enable mentorship and accountability, making the daunting prospect of early morning runs more approachable and enjoyable.

One of the most remarkable outcomes was an interdepartmental dialogue that had been missing in the formal confines of the office. Running side by side, executives and interns shared personal stories, professional advice and even brainstormed projects, leading to innovative ideas that might never have emerged in a traditional meeting-room setting.

The initiative also caught the attention of the company's leadership, who saw the value in promoting employee

well-being. They started to support the running club officially, offering resources like professional trainers and nutri-
tion workshops, and sponsoring participation in external
marathons. This acknowledgement from the upper
echelons of the company not only boosted the club's profile
but also highlighted the importance of health and wellness
in the corporate ethos.

What if you started a mentorship programme or peer-
to-peer learning sessions where knowledge and skills are
exchanged freely? This will not only improve your own
skills but also create a more connected and supportive workplace environment. The more you connect with
others, the stronger the community you can build in the
workplace.

Here are some of the key ways you can enhance your
workplace experience as a professional.

1. CREATE NETWORKING OPPORTUNITIES

Organize or participate in networking events within your
workplace. These can be formal events like seminars and
workshops, or informal gatherings like coffee meet-ups and
lunch-and-learn sessions. These events provide a platform
to connect with colleagues, share knowledge and develop
professional relationships.

2. TEAM-BUILDING ACTIVITIES

Engage in team-building activities that are not just work-
related. These could include volunteer work, sports activities

or cultural events. These activities can improve communication, boost team morale, and create a more cohesive workplace environment.

3. ENABLE FEEDBACK AND AN INCLUSIVE CULTURE

Prioritize a culture where feedback is valued and inclusivity is a priority. Encourage open dialogue, respect diverse viewpoints, and create an environment where every employee feels valued and heard. This can lead to a more innovative workplace culture.

4. MENTORSHIP PROGRAMMES

Participate in or establish a mentorship programme. Being a mentor or a mentee can be a rewarding experience. It's an opportunity to share experiences, learn new perspectives and develop leadership skills.

Asif Farook is the Senior Programme Manager at the University of Hertfordshire, supporting the local entrepreneurial ecosystem including student start-ups and helping companies innovate and de-risk their innovation by accessing university expertise, facilities and public funding. I spoke to him about the benefits of mentorship in his career.

'In my early thirties I did a course called "Leading through Coaching". I had a mentor who worked with me, and taught me the art of mindful listening, how to be present in conversation and listen intently. The course and mentor had a very positive impact on both my professional and personal life. I still to this day hear her voice in my mind, asking "Are you listening intently?"'

Mentorship can have an impact on an individual's growth. Asif's experience of learning mindful listening and being present in conversations from a mentor shows the power of effective mentorship. Such skills are not only essential for leadership and coaching but also invaluable in everyday interactions, enhancing your ability to communicate, empathize, and connect with others on a deeper level.

Sam Jennings, who mentors me personally, offered some further insight on the importance of mentorship. Sam has been instrumental in the growth of Clarion Events over the last ten years, delivering more than thirty M&A (mergers and acquisitions) transactions. He describes it as a privilege to have spent such a large amount of time getting to know entrepreneurs all over the world, hearing their stories and understanding their business models. These interactions have given Sam a unique insight into how new and fast-growing B2B media businesses are doing things differently, in particular around teams, culture, data, content and use of technology.

In 2022, Sam set up Opus Origin with a group of investors and is now focused on bringing together a portfolio of high-performing B2B media and events businesses. 'I love mentoring, in the same way I love coaching the sport I love. It helps me to realize the depth of my knowledge and the value that it can bring to different scenarios. It makes me more effective by realizing the power of enabling growth in others.'

We then talked about his experience mentoring me. '[It] has developed so much in such a short space of time. You've gone from an employee/part-time entrepreneur to an independent entrepreneur, running a business with a number of employees. I would like to think I have helped you with the way you manage and operate your business, giving you confidence to make big decisions and optimizing the business for growth through our highly objective discussions.'

For me, Sam's guidance has been incredibly valuable. He doesn't just give me advice, he also gives me the confidence to make big decisions on my own. Sam teaches me in a way that helps me think carefully about my choices, showing me it's not just about doing what I'm told but also learning to stand on my own two feet. Mentorship is more than just giving instructions; it's about helping someone grow so much that they eventually don't need your help.

A relationship with a mentor helps you become more confident, encourages you to keep learning and prepares you to tackle challenges with a clear head. Mentorship helps mould future leaders who can handle complex situations with ease and creativity. Essentially, a good mentor helps you become independent and ready to make your own mark in the world.

Mentorship extends beyond the transfer of specific skills or knowledge. It involves the shaping of our approach to interactions and a heightened awareness of how we engage with others. The lasting influence of the mentor – as shown by the fact the words of Asif's mentor echo in his mind so many years later – exemplifies the enduring value of mentor–mentee relationships. Mentors can leave a lasting imprint on our lives, guiding us long after direct interactions have ceased.

Reflect with Raphael

- *What activities or initiatives could you start or participate in to create greater camaraderie among your colleagues?*
- *How could you contribute to a mentorship programme or a peer-to-peer learning session in your workplace?*
- *What types of events or interactions could you initiate or get involved in that would expand your professional network internally?*

Creating a Cohesive Team

There is a well-known quote from John C. Maxwell: 'Leadership is not about titles, positions, or flow charts. It is about one life influencing another.'[10] As a manager or leader, your ability to create a cohesive team is critical for the success of your company. Your influence profoundly shapes the organization's culture, setting the tone for future progress.

As my own company continues to grow, being able to create a cohesive and thriving company culture becomes of even more importance to me. Our mission and vision is to inspire Black entrepreneurs, professionals, and allies to create change. Lasting change that sees us level the playing field, create progress and development for our community to thrive. Everything we do is aligned with that company mission and vision.

As a leader, it is imperative that you master the art of conveying and embodying a vision that not only captivates the members of your team but also encompasses the aspirations and values of every individual within the company. At the start of every year, I run through the company vision, both for the new starters and as a refresher for the people who were already here.

Each team member needs to be fully engaged and aligned with the overarching objectives of the company. Research has shown that in companies with highly engaged teams there is a 21 per cent increase in profitability.[11] Effective leadership is key to harmonizing individual efforts towards collective triumph.

Transparent communication and regular feedback are also very important; these are key to building a foundation of trust and understanding within your team. Research consistently shows that open communication in the workplace leads to improved job satisfaction, productivity and employee engagement.

Once a month, I set aside time with each member of my team. It's an opportunity for them to be honest and transparent with me, and I ask them about how they are finding the company, what improvements they would like to see, and if there is anything challenging them or anything else they would like to discuss. For me it's important to create this space as feedback is invaluable, and transparency can only benefit the business. This does not mean that I will action everything they suggest, but allowing my team to speak their minds without fear has been hugely beneficial. In fact, it has helped me to come up with new ideas, solve internal problems, and challenged me to do things better.

When you ensure each team member feels that they are heard and their contributions are valued, it keeps morale high and creates a positive work environment. This not only enhances team dynamics but also drives better performance, as employees are more engaged and committed to achieving shared goals.

Karen Wardle described how she implements open communication and encourages regular feedback in her team. 'Being open for me is key to being an effective leader. Having worked for leaders in the past who have not been open in their communication, it left me feeling disengaged, not truly understanding our team's purpose or knowing what was expected of me. As a leader of teams, I have made a conscious effort to be open, communicate our purpose, align on our values and ensure team members understand how their role fits into the goals and ambitions of the business we are supporting.

'Importantly, I don't pretend to have all the answers – I seek team members' views and input, ensuring they feel empowered and confident to contribute. I share feedback in the moment, both positive and constructive, enabling colleagues to reflect and respond. I seek feedback from my team and ensure I make time for them through regular 1:1s. It's important to me that they know I have their back and will champion and support them. To do that I ask them to look through the lens of "no surprises" – no matter how big or small, timely communication is key to enable us to grow as individuals and a team, and having aligned values gives us a foundation to communicate from.'

Karen's commitment to transparency and inclusivity in communication practices is instrumental to preventing feelings of disengagement and confusion among her team when it comes to their direction and individual roles. By clearly articulating the team's purpose and making sure they all align on shared values, Karen ensures that every member of her team understands their contribution to the broader business goals.

A key strategy she implements is the democratization of idea generation and decision-making processes. Recognizing that effective leadership involves humility and teamwork, Karen actively seeks input from her team members, empowering them to voice their opinions and suggestions. This approach not only enriches the decision-making process with diverse perspectives but also boosts team members' confidence in their value to the group.

Feedback, both positive and constructive, is shared promptly and directly, promoting a culture of continuous improvement and adaptability. This practice of giving feedback in the moment encourages immediate reflection and growth, making it a powerful tool for personal and professional development. Similarly, Karen's openness to receiving feedback underscores the reciprocal nature of communication. Regular one-on-one meetings are prioritized, providing a dedicated space for individualized attention, support and feedback exchange.

The concept of 'no surprises' communication further solidifies the team's foundation of trust and mutual respect.

By encouraging timely sharing of information, regardless of its significance, Karen ensures that challenges and achievements are collectively addressed.

In his book *Work Rules!*, Laszlo Bock touches on the importance of a high-trust environment. He suggests that in settings where employees feel empowered to express ideas and concerns without fear of repercussions, it leads to innovative and bold problem-solving.[12] When leaders cultivate an environment where every idea, no matter how small, is valued and considered, they can unlock the full potential of their team's collective intelligence.

Reflect with Raphael

- *What strategies can I employ to ensure that each team member feels heard and their contributions are valued?*
- *How might assigning roles that play to each team member's strengths while also challenging them to grow help build a more dynamic and resilient team?*
- *How can I articulate and demonstrate a vision that is both inspiring and inclusive, ensuring that every member of the organization feels aligned with its goals and values?*

Creating a Positive and Collaborative Work Environment

Building a thriving community is not a one-off task but a continuous process that involves a thoughtful blend of strategic initiatives and cultural shifts. As Simon Sinek, a renowned leadership expert, has said: 'A team is not a group of people who work together. A team is a group of people who trust each other.'[13] This statement describes the essence of a thriving workplace community: it's about moving beyond mere cooperation to genuine support and teamwork.

Creating a positive and collaborative work environment involves a blend of strategies that can revolutionize the way a business operates and interacts internally. Here are four effective strategies.

1. ENCOURAGE TEAM-BUILDING AND COLLABORATION

Strong relationships and a sense of unity among employees is key. This can be achieved through various team-building activities. Rondette Amoy Smith, Global Director of Equity, Inclusion & Diversity at Tapestry, a global house of iconic brands, is a passionate and impact-driven diversity and inclusion leader. As an expert and thought leader in this field, she advocates for a hands-on approach and a keen focus on stakeholder engagement, enabling the empowerment of internal talent and effective management. She is also the founder and co-host of *Race2Rise* – a podcast focusing on the experiences of two Black female expatriates that centres around empowering women of colour to engage in discussions on challenging topics such as navigating the workplace, mental health, owning and pursuing their passion and purpose, and developing strong networks and healthy relationships.

Rondette shared some unique and unconventional team-building activities that have impacted her team's dynamic. 'One of the most memorable team-building exercises I've done with either clients or my very own teams is an icebreaker called "The Last Concert". I give full credit to one of my dearest friends who introduced me to it at the beginning of my career. He worked at an education non-profit and said it was quite a hit amongst his teams.

'I was hesitant to replicate the icebreaker at work (after all, I worked in banking at the time, which often has a reputation for being more serious than fun), but after giving it some thought, I decided to go for it, and I've continued to use it for every team-building session ever since. The concept is pretty simple – it's your last day on earth and your very own personal concert will be organized for you and only you. You get a thirty-minute opening act, a two-hour main act and a one-hour closing set. It can be a singer, a comedian, a dancer, a politician or other famous figure – past or present.

'Much to my surprise, people always love this activity, and most importantly it provides such amazing insight into an individual's preferences, passions and purpose. For example, who would've thought that a senior executive from Germany in her early sixties would've chosen Pink for her main act? Or that a new analyst who had recently matriculated from the graduate programme would insist on grooving to The Temptations to close out his concert?

'What this icebreaker really demonstrates is the power of creating a safe space to share intimate and personal details about one another. It enables teams to share a sense of community by realizing that they're probably more alike than different and that there are probably preconceived assumptions they carry about one another when really there's beauty in taking the time to slow down and truly get to know and understand one another.

'Team dynamics don't happen or thrive by chance, but through intentional growth and engagement and a true focus and desire on thriving together as a community.'

The Last Concert icebreaker exemplifies an innovative approach to team-building that goes beyond conventional activities, showing how unique and seemingly unconventional exercises can create deeper connections among team members. This particular activity, despite its initial morbid premise, ingeniously opens up a space for individuals to share personal tastes and interests in a fun, imaginative setting. The choice of three different groups or performers from any genre or era offers a broad canvas for expression, revealing layers of personality and preferences that might not surface in everyday work interactions.

People's surprise and delight in discovering unexpected choices demonstrates the activity's effectiveness in breaking down preconceived notions and stereotypes within the team. Such revelations not only serve as conversation starters but also highlight the diverse interests and backgrounds that each team member brings to the table. This diversity, when celebrated and understood, can significantly enrich team dynamics, creating a stronger sense of unity.

The success of this activity in a banking environment, traditionally perceived as serious, shows the universal appeal of engaging, personal storytelling activities in building rapport among colleagues. It demonstrates that creating a safe space for sharing personal stories and interests can be a powerful tool in developing a cohesive team culture, regardless of the industry.

2. RECOGNIZE AND REWARD EMPLOYEE ACHIEVEMENTS

Acknowledging and celebrating employee accomplishments is essential for boosting morale, motivation and engagement. This can be done through public recognition, awards, bonuses and promotions. Implementing peer-to-peer recognition programmes can also help create a supportive work culture, as employees feel valued by both their colleagues and managers.

3. PROVIDE OPPORTUNITIES FOR PROFESSIONAL DEVELOPMENT

Opportunities for professional growth are vital for employee job satisfaction and loyalty. This includes joining professional groups, attending networking events, online courses, formal education, conferences, management and leadership training, and obtaining professional certifications. These opportunities demonstrate an organization's commitment to employee growth and development, leading to a more engaged and loyal workforce.

4. PROMOTE WORK–LIFE BALANCE AND WELL-BEING

A healthy balance between work and personal life is essential for employees in order to maintain well-being and perform at their best. Strategies to promote work–life balance include setting realistic schedules, focusing on employee well-being, providing resources for mental and physical health, training in attention management skills, establishing clear expectations around working hours, and offering flexible work arrangements. A culture of trust and respect is also crucial, especially in an environment where staff are working from home.

These strategies require a thoughtful approach and an understanding that creating a positive work environment is more than just the physical space; it's about promoting employee well-being, productivity, growth and a culture of trust.

Reflect with Raphael

- *How do you perceive the role of trust within your team, and in what ways can you actively contribute to building trust among your employees and/or colleagues?*
- *Think about ways you can recognize and reward employee achievements.*
- *Consider the importance of professional development opportunities. How do you prioritize your own growth within your career, and what steps could your*

organization take to better support this aspect of employee satisfaction?

- *Reflect on your current work–life balance. What strategies do you find most effective in maintaining this balance, and how could your workplace improve its support for employee well-being, particularly in remote working scenarios?*

Cultivating Inclusivity and Diversity

A McKinsey study found that companies in the top quartile for racial and ethnic diversity were 35 per cent more likely to have financial returns above their respective national industry medians.[14] Just to be clear, diversity and inclusion is the right thing to do, but from a financial perspective it can also be very beneficial to your company. So, what do you have to lose?

It's not just about having diverse perspectives present but making sure they are actively valued and leveraged when it comes to decision-making and innovation. This is summed up well in this insightful quote: 'Diversity is being invited to the party; inclusion is being asked to dance.'[15]

Harvard Business Review research indicates that companies with higher-than-average diversity had 19 per cent higher innovation revenues.[16] A commitment to diversity and inclusion helps with ground-breaking ideas and solutions, and there is a direct link between a diverse workforce and the ability to generate marketable innovative products and services.

The challenge always lies in integrating diversity into the fabric of an organization's culture, going beyond recruitment to influence policies, practices and everyday interactions.

Reflect with Raphael

- *Reflect on your organization's approach to diversity and inclusion. Are diverse perspectives genuinely influencing and enriching the decision-making process?*
- *In what ways could a more diverse and inclusive environment unlock untapped creative potential, leading to enhanced innovation and market responsiveness in your business?*
- *What concrete steps are you taking to ensure that your diversity initiatives are not just performative, but rather truly transformative, creating an environment where every individual feels valued and empowered to contribute their unique perspectives and skills?*
- *How can your organization move from simply recognizing the importance of diversity and inclusion to actively living and breathing these values every day?*

Community and Career Advancement

A *Harvard Business Review* study revealed that 85 per cent of professionals attribute major career progression to their workplace networks,[17] highlighting that each interaction has the potential for new learning, opportunities and pathways for growth.

As Reid Hoffman, the co-founder of LinkedIn, eloquently puts it: 'Your network is the people who want to help you, and you want to help them, and that's really powerful.' This symbiotic relationship within a thriving community is not just about individual development but also collective success.

Enhanced Networking Opportunities

Involvement in a workplace community can be a game-changer when it comes to expanding your professional network – a key factor in unlocking new and exciting career opportunities.

The act of engaging with peers, participating in group activities and contributing to community discussions does more than just add names to a contact list; it builds connections that can pave the way for future career advancements.

Cecil Peters told me how he managed to land his current role at JPMorgan: 'My current role is Head of Diversity, Equity and Inclusion across all of EMEA. However I did not have a HR or DEI background beforehand. I have had a long career as a technologist, from operations to software engineering and programme management to enterprise sales. However, when I joined JPMorgan Chase, I was able to volunteer my spare time to network with the Advancing Black Pathways team in the US, using my technology experience to address some of the challenges facing the Black community, particularly Black business owners.

'Through the work I did, Advancing Black Pathways saw the potential that I had as a DEI practitioner, and offered me a full-time role, running the function across EMEA. Following a very successful first year running Advancing Black Pathways, I was then asked to run DEI across all of EMEA. These opportunities would not have availed themselves to me if I had not been willing to put my spare time and energy into someone else's good cause.'

Cecil's journey from a technologist to becoming the EMEA Head of Diversity, Equity and Inclusion at a major firm exemplifies how voluntary engagement with internal networks can lead to unexpected and significant career opportunities. By volunteering with the Advancing Black Pathways team, he leveraged his technology experience to make meaningful contributions to initiatives addressing challenges faced by the Black community, including Black business owners. This proactive engagement not only showed he was able to apply his skills in new contexts, but also highlighted his potential as a DEI practitioner. His experience is a testament to how workplace networks can serve as platforms for demonstrating your value and how you align with broader organizational goals, beyond the confines of formal job roles.

Organizations place a huge amount of value on employees who are willing to invest their time and energy in causes that advance the company's mission and contribute to societal good. Networking and active participation in workplace communities or groups can uncover hidden opportunities for career advancement, especially when employees demonstrate a commitment to leveraging their skills for the benefit of the wider community.

Data from a LinkedIn survey revealed that in 2016 a staggering 70 per cent of individuals were hired at companies where they had an existing connection.[18] This shows the critical role that networking plays in a professional community – not only in terms of uncovering job openings but also in facilitating the transition into these roles. The value of these connections lies in their quality; it's about ensuring the relationships are mutually beneficial, and that both parties can offer support, advice and opportunities to each other.

It's essential to think of networking not as a numbers game, but as a strategic effort to build relationships that can support and enhance your professional journey.

CHAPTER 5

Nurturing Meaningful Relationships for Self-Development

Nurturing meaningful relationships has never been more crucial for self-development.

Finding and nurturing your tribe is more than a social endeavour; it's a vital component to your personal development journey. People are the components in this world that can bring the best and the worst out of you, and if you engage in the right relationships, you can really utilize them to help you become the best version of yourself. It's relationships with people and the connections I have made that have helped me tap into different character traits I never knew I had.

Building and sustaining relationships not only enriches our lives but also enhances our personal growth. Brené Brown has eloquently stated that 'connection is why we're here; it gives purpose and meaning to our lives'. Our interpersonal connections are a powerful tool when it comes to self-discovery and personal evolution.

Mike Sealy, Vice President of Diversity, Equity and Inclusion at Informa Markets, a world-leading exhibition and event organizer, is a British leader with a strong client-centric and customer-experience mindset, and demonstrable experience of leading teams across complex international matrixed organizations. When we talked, he touched on why he believes interpersonal communications are so important.

'I treat all interpersonal connections as a learning opportunity. Sometimes a single comment or thought will stick with me and provide the opportunity to do something in a different way or even spark a new idea. This is one of the reasons why I am continually increasing my network and connections because it serves as a vehicle for continuous learning, self-discovery and personal evolution.'

By perceiving every interaction as a potential learning opportunity, Mike maintains a mindset that is inherently open and growth-oriented. Such a perspective not only values the diversity of human experiences and viewpoints but also recognizes the potential in every conversation to inspire change, whether by altering existing perspectives, introducing new methodologies or sparking innovative ideas.

Personal evolution is enriched by the myriad voices and stories encountered through social interaction. Each connection, regardless of its duration or initial impact, is a valuable contributor to your understanding and development.

Mac Alonge is an impact-focused leader with 15+ years' experience advising some of the world's leading organizations. As CEO of data-driven equality, diversity and inclusion (EDI) consultancy The Equal Group, Mac leads a multidisciplinary team delivering EDI transformation projects to companies across public, private and voluntary sectors. Before founding his award-winning consultancy, Mac spent ten years as a regulatory consultant, focusing on energy and utilities, and worked for organizations such as KPMG, the National Grid and the UK government.

Mac is determined to nurture varied relationships for his own self-development. He told me: 'I've always been interested in establishing relationships with those that have a different context to me, usually along the lines of race, age and gender. Gaining from these different perspectives has often taken me on a journey of broadening my own horizons and understanding more about the world as experienced by different people.

'I try to be as intentional as possible in seeking out different views, but am most conscious of other entrepreneurs, with a focus on those that are at a similar stage to myself, as well as those that are further ahead (i.e. where I'd like to be in 3–5 years' time). For those that are at a similar stage as me, the substance of the relationship comes from having people around that know what you're going through and can empathize. The relationships tend to be mutually beneficial and are very practical around problem-solving and provide opportunities to think about challenges in a different way. With those that are further along on their journey, I'm often seeking inspiration and a deeper understanding of how to navigate issues over the long term. The stories and wisdom shared by those further ahead have been an invaluable source of inspiration and personal development.

I've also received a lot of challenge and critique from these relationships, which has often caused me to reflect on my approaches.

'Around the time of George Floyd's murder I was put in contact with an amazing ally and advocate who had been working in the diversity and inclusion space for several years, and we were sharing our respective journeys and challenges – our relationship quickly developed trust and vulnerability. As I shared in more detail some of the business challenges that I was facing, she suggested that I speak to her husband to see if there was any value he could add, so we connected and I found the conversation to be enriching and uplifting. As an entrepreneur it can be hard to find the time to step back and take stock of where you are and how much you've achieved, whether you feel like it or not. Our conversations turned into a more formal mentoring relationship, with regular time to catch up and break down some of the challenges I'm facing, and in some cases, the challenges that he's facing.'

Engaging with peers at a similar entrepreneurial stage offers space for mutual empathy and practical support. These relationships become an opportunity for shared learning, where problem-solving and innovative thinking flourish through the exchange of ideas and experiences. The reciprocity in these connections ensures that both parties benefit, forming an environment that is helpful for navigating the immediate challenges of entrepreneurship.

Conversely, relationships with more experienced entrepreneurs serve as a source of inspiration and guidance. Mentors not just provide a glimpse into potential future paths but also offer critical insights and advice for the long term. The value of shared stories and wisdom cannot be overstated, as they are invaluable resources for inspiration, strategy and resilience. Any critique and challenges from these seasoned entrepreneurs should prompt reflective thinking, encouraging a re-evaluation of strategy and approach in light of their broader experiences and success.

There is vulnerability and trust involved in building these relationships. With Mac, the trust and vulnerability he developed in his relationship with an ally in the diversity and inclusion space led to a further enriching connection, showcasing the unexpected avenues through which support and guidance can emerge. The fact this evolved into a formal mentoring dynamic emphasizes the importance of regular, reflective discussions that not only address immediate challenges but also look towards long-term achievements and ongoing obstacles.

There are so many complexities to modern relationships; there is a delicate balance between self-care, empathy, and learning how to give without losing yourself in the process. I want to challenge you to reflect on your own relationships. How do they shape your identity and your path towards self-fulfilment?

Self-Awareness and Personal Growth

The influence of community on our personal development has not just been casually observed, it has been extensively studied and documented. In their seminal work 'Sense of Community', David McMillan and David Chavis emphasize the impact on individuals of belonging and mutual commitment. According to their research, it's the belonging that is vital for personal development, providing a safe space for self-exploration and growth.[19]

Annisha Taylor, however, challenges McMillan and Chavis's conclusions. Head of Diversity & Inclusion at the BBC, specializing in the creation of distinctive organizational strategies that promote inclusivity, champion diversity and address inequalities, Annisha understands the importance of cultivating environments that enable individuals and teams to perform, thrive and grow. 'Perhaps somewhat controversially, I have mixed sentiments about McMillan and Chavis's theory that a sense of community is "a feeling that members have of belonging". Ultimately, individuals need to feel welcomed and equipped with an environment that enables them to do their best work. I personally don't see the need to "belong". What I see as more crucial is the ability for an individual to feel they will be accepted when bringing whichever version of themself into that community, without fear of reprisal.'

Annisha's insight highlights the importance of creating inclusive environments that prioritize acceptance over the traditional notion of belonging. Communities should be spaces where diversity of thought, identity and expression is not just tolerated but embraced. This approach creates a culture of openness and encourages members to engage fully and genuinely, contributing to the richness and dynamism of the community. Annisha is inviting a re-evaluation of what it means to be part of a community, suggesting that the true measure of a community's strength lies in its capacity to create an environment of acceptance and authenticity.

Communities offer a diverse array of perspectives, beliefs and experiences, an environment that allows self-awareness to flourish. They provide a reflective surface, a kind of social mirror, which reveals to us aspects of our character and behaviour that are often invisible when we are alone. In essence, we need other people to help us discover who we really are.

Psychologist Abraham Maslow, in his Hierarchy of Needs theory, describes belonging as a precursor to self-actualization.[20] In the communal context, this belonging goes beyond mere acceptance, morphing into a dynamic interaction where personal insights are gleaned through the process of social exchange. Community involvement can have a huge impact on an individual's understanding of themselves, and engaging in activities often challenges us to step out of our comfort zones, confront our biases and develop empathy for others.

Here are some of the key ways that nurturing meaningful relationships helps to serve us in self-awareness and personal growth.

Mentorship, Guidance and Knowledge-Sharing

Having a strong community within the workplace is often linked to opportunities for mentorship, a key ingredient in the recipe for career success and development.

Florence Henderson discussed with me why mentorship was instrumental for her: 'I had the opportunity to participate in an external programme and to select an executive sponsor, and I chose a past manager. He took his "sponsorship" seriously and guided me through the programme – always focused on what I wanted to achieve from participating and how it would help to accelerate my professional growth.

'At the end of the programme the conversations continued, and he has been able to mentor me through different scenarios and make me think about my future plans, both personally and professionally. My executive sponsor has influenced my professional development by having the ability *to hear what I'm not saying* and in helping me to build my confidence.'

A thoughtful and engaged mentor can significantly influence an individual's career trajectory, and so it is important to choose a mentor who is genuinely invested in your growth. Florence selected a past manager as an executive sponsor, and this mentor's approach, characterized by a deep commitment to Florence's goals and providing continuous guidance, is a remarkable example of effective mentorship. Their emphasis on growth speaks volumes about their leadership and mentoring philosophy, echoing a belief that professional environments should be conducive to development. By focusing on Florence's aspirations and providing tailored advice through various professional scenarios, the mentor played a key role in shaping Florence's future. This level of personalized guidance was crucial in helping Florence navigate the complexities of career planning, objective-setting, networking and business travel.

Moreover, her mentor's ability to listen to what was *not* being said is a testament to the depth of the mentor–mentee relationship. It indicates a level of empathy and understanding that goes beyond surface-level interactions, allowing for a more nuanced and supportive mentorship experience. Such a relationship not only built up Florence's confidence but also equipped her with the insights and strategies needed to make informed decisions about her career path.

Florence's relationship with her mentor highlights that the quality of mentorship can have an impact on professional growth. Effective mentorship requires more than just a title or position; there must be a genuine commitment to the mentee's success and an understanding of their unique needs and goals.

A study published in the *Harvard Business Review* found that a striking 84 per cent of top executives credited mentors with helping them avoid expensive mistakes and attain proficiency in their roles, highlighting that mentors can act as a springboard in shaping the career trajectories of their mentees.[21]

In a rapidly changing business landscape, staying up-to-date with the latest skills and knowledge can be challenging for individuals. Within a strong professional community, you will have access to a diverse pool of knowledge and perspectives, which can be instrumental in keeping you abreast of new trends and technologies.

Emotional and Psychological Support

Emotional support from colleagues and superiors is the antidote to the pressures of the modern work environment. The American Psychological Association reports that employees who feel supported by their workplace community experience substantially less job-related stress. In fact, 56 per cent of workers in supportive environments report higher levels of motivation and commitment to their roles.[22]

Emotional support in the workplace is not just about reducing stress; it's also about empowering employees to take calculated risks and embrace change – both key drivers of innovation and career progression.

Another aspect worth pondering is how emotional support can help individuals navigate career or business transitions. When a company faces restructuring or an employee is considering a career pivot, the support of a community can be crucial. An analysis by the Society for Human Resource Management found that employees who felt supported during organizational changes were more likely to remain with the company and adjust successfully to new roles or processes.[23]

Building Emotional Intelligence
through Social Interactions

Regular interaction with a diverse group of individuals in different settings can significantly boost your emotional intelligence. Learning to deal with different personalities, manage conflicts and build meaningful relationships are all aspects of emotional intelligence that can be developed through involvement with communities.

Florence Henderson spoke about how being part of a community has helped her build emotional intelligence, particularly when it comes to managing conflicts and building relationships. 'To me, emotional intelligence is about empathy, communicating effectively, helping others relieve their stress and defusing conflict. Work has afforded me a community that I spend a lot of time with, and through my role as the Inclusion Lead across Europe, the Middle East, Africa and the Asia-Pacific region, I have been able to be a source of trust and support where needed. Building relationships can take time; but showing emotional intelligence can really make all the difference in helping someone feel heard and giving them a sense of belonging.'

It becomes evident that emotional intelligence – characterized by empathy, effective communication, stress relief and conflict diffusion – is not just a personal asset but a communal one. The workplace, as a community, is an environment where these aspects of emotional intelligence are continuously in play, and they are critical for creating a supportive and inclusive culture.

Moreover, the ability to communicate effectively and help others relieve stress play a vital role in defusing potential conflicts. In a diverse workplace community, where differing perspectives exist and potential misunderstandings may arise, emotional intelligence is the key to navigating these challenges smoothly. It enables leaders and team members alike to approach conflicts with a mindset geared towards resolution and mutual understanding rather than confrontation.

Accountability and Support

Being part of a community often means having people who support you in your goals and hold you accountable. This can be especially beneficial for personal growth, as it encourages you to stay committed to your self-development and provides a support network when you are facing challenges.

Scarlett Allen-Horton is a highly accomplished recruitment leader, a finalist on BBC's *The Apprentice*, an innovative entrepreneur and a founder of the multi-award-winning Harper Fox Search Partners. She spoke about an experience of having a community that supported her. 'After my incident I spent the first two years calling and debating whether to go to this domestic abuse charity. I sat down and instantly thought, *Should I be here? This is definitely not for me, what on earth am I doing here?* I quickly realized that every other woman in the room understood me. A true community of understanding sitting amongst each other, not knowing each other, not even wanting to look up at each other, but a community that all shared very similar experiences – a knowing, an understanding, a togetherness.'

Supporting others within a community is a journey of self-discovery and growth. Earning new perspectives and building confidence contribute significantly to your personal development.

Cultural and Social Awareness

A community, particularly one that is diverse, enhances cultural and social awareness. This heightened awareness is a crucial aspect of self-development, helping to create a more inclusive and empathetic world view.

CHAPTER 6

Social Community and Its Impact on Well-Being

Well-being is a theme that is both timeless and increasingly relevant in today's fast-paced world.

Renowned psychologist Carl Jung once noted, 'The meeting of two personalities is like the contact of two chemical substances: if there is any reaction, both are transformed.'[24] This insight captures the essence of how social connections are not just interactions but experiences that significantly impact our mental health.

Our workplaces often come with inherent pressures and structured interactions, but it's the cultivation of social networks in personal spheres that offers an avenue for emotional support and authentic connection.

Social communities, especially those outside of professional settings, reveal a complex yet rewarding landscape. They offer a sanctuary where individuals can seek solace, understanding and genuine connection away from the rigours of their work life. These non-professional communities, ranging from hobby groups to volunteer organizations and even friend groups, can significantly contribute to your sense of identity and self-worth.

Understanding the Importance of Social Connections for Mental Health

A study by the American Psychological Association reveals that individuals with strong social ties exhibit lower levels of stress and depression, enhancing their overall mental resilience.[25] This finding is particularly salient in the context of building supportive social communities outside of work environments.

Khalia Ismain explained to me how having a strong social support network as an entrepreneur helps her cope with stress and improves her mental resilience: 'Building a business is incredibly hard – you believe so strongly in what you are doing and it's natural to see your business as an extension of you, rising and falling with every success and failure. It took me two years before I realized how detrimental that was to my mental health, and I actively took steps to address it. Through speaking to other founders I recognized and accepted how normal my emotional experience was. I called my mum regularly, ensured I continued to meet up socially with my friends, and had a weekly bubble bath! By taking a step back and prioritizing myself, I ensured that I was able to mentally cope with the stresses of being a founder in the long run.'

The journey of entrepreneurship is often deeply personal, with the highs and lows of the business directly impacting a founder's emotional and mental well-being. The realization that maintaining mental health is just as important as business success was an important step for Khalia.

The proactive steps she took to address mental health – engaging in conversations with fellow founders, maintaining close contact with family, and ensuring social interactions with friends – emphasize the multifaceted nature of a person's support networks. These networks provide not only emotional validation and perspective but also practical strategies for stress management and self-care. For Khalia, calling her mother provided emotional support and grounding, while social outings with friends offered a necessary escape and a reminder of life outside the business. Additionally, it is important to set aside time for relaxation, mental rest and personal rituals, such as a weekly bubble bath.

The fact that other founders were encountering the same challenges as Khalia is a reminder that the emotional rollercoaster of entrepreneurship is a common journey. Speaking to others in the same position offered solace and normalized the stress and challenges she was facing. This kind of support is crucial in mitigating feelings of isolation and overwhelm, and encountering a shared understanding can significantly bolster your mental resilience.

Kanya King MBE also talked about how social communities can provide safe spaces for discussing mental health issues. 'We've partnered with charities like Help Musicians to offer resources and support for mental health, emphasizing the importance of destigmatizing mental health issues and promoting diversity and inclusion to foster a sense of belonging.'

The Harvard Study of Adult Development, one of the longest studies of adult life, found that close relationships, more than money or fame, are what keep people happy throughout their lives.[26] This research challenges the conventional metrics of success and happiness.

Renowned psychologist Susan Pinker has said: 'Face-to-face contact releases a whole cascade of neurotransmitters and, like a vaccine, they protect you now, in the present, and well into the future.'[27] This comparison is particularly poignant, illustrating that these interactions serve as a protective measure, fortifying our mental resilience not just in the immediate aftermath of an encounter but long into the future. In an increasingly digital and fast-paced world, in-person conversations and human connections are irreplaceable. Loneliness and social isolation are on the rise, reminding us of the value of personal interactions in safeguarding our mental health.

In Mac Alonge's opinion, 'It comes down to each individual and their context. As someone who is perhaps a bit older and grew up in a world without mobile phones and still remembers using pay phones and arranging to meet friends at a time and place with the only option being to wait at said time and place until they arrived – I much prefer face-to-face interactions. I believe there is so much energy that you can gain from being in and around people when interacting.

'My work requires me to do a lot of training, facilitation, presenting and speaking, and again, the energy you get from being in the room is unmatched. Cues around body language and engagement levels are a lot easier to gauge, which means that you know when to change gears or alter your approach. During the pandemic I think we got so used to Zoom meetings and probably took for granted how easily we could "connect" with people.

'I think the digital experience of connecting is an extension of what we see on social media with people masking and putting on a show, or even putting out the image that they want the world to see of them, i.e. perfectly curated backdrops and/or being smartly dressed from the waist up, while wearing jogging bottoms or shorts – it's a lot harder to mask or present a fictional view of yourself in person. I think this leads to being more authentic and honest in person, which gives the other person or people licence to do the same. In terms of the impact on mental health, although it sounds weird, seeing other people's struggles, battles and challenges makes us feel human in our own struggles, battles and challenges, whereas social media encourages us to focus on people's highlight reels, which can convince us that we are not enough or not achieving by comparison.'

Prioritizing your mental health is so key; the mind is the invisible part of our body that, if damaged, can be just as fatal as an injury to a visible part of our body – if not worse. This is backed up by statistics from the Office of the US Surgeon General, which suggest that loneliness and social isolation can be as damaging to health as smoking fifteen cigarettes a day, highlighting the need for deep, authentic connections.[28]

Rondette Amoy Smith shared with me some effective ways to combat loneliness and social isolation: 'Shortly after I had my daughter, I found myself in a deeply isolating situation – far away from family and my closest friends with very limited ability to travel to see and spend time with them. Prior to becoming a mum, I was a carefree expat, so moments of loneliness were often remedied by attending networking events, hanging out with fellow expats and non-stop jet-setting, but there was something supremely grounding about becoming a parent for me. I had no family support in London, and I yearned for the care and compassion of my tribe. After several months of enduring this intense isolation, I began to notice the impact on my well-being – sleeping patterns, mood, weight fluctuations and downtrodden spirits.

'I knew I had to shift my perspective to rise out of the space I was in, but I won't lie – it was extremely challenging, particularly with other forces against me. Slowly, I began to recall what used to bring me joy. Of course, my daughter was central to my joy, but I had to remember that I was a whole, happy and successful person before being blessed with her. I started forcing myself to get outdoors for long walks. I found my faith again and began praying and meditating daily as well as fasting with purpose weekly. I continued to engage proactively in therapy. I ate healthier meals and took up reformer pilates again. And I welcomed it when my friends and family back home set up Zoom calls just to talk, listen or laugh.

'There's an old saying, "no man is an island", and it's so true. If you find yourself in a situation where you feel intense loneliness or social isolation, know it won't be for ever. Acknowledge the feeling, share with someone you trust, and devise a game plan with your tribe and community for both maintaining and enhancing your mental health that will enable you to regain your sense of self.'

The isolation Rondette felt after the shift from leading an active, socially engaged expat life to becoming a mother highlights how drastic changes in your social environment can lead to unexpected feelings of loneliness. Her journey towards overcoming this isolation demonstrates the importance of proactive self-care and community support. Rediscovering joy through activities that previously brought happiness and fulfilment is a crucial strategy in addressing the effects of loneliness. It not only helps to alleviate the immediate symptoms of isolation, but also contributes to reclaiming your identity and overall well-being.

Acknowledging feelings of loneliness, reaching out for support, and actively engaging in practices that foster mental and physical health are vital steps in navigating yourself out of isolation.

Building a community is about creating connections with the right people, and finding your tribe is a step towards psychological resilience and emotional fulfilment. These connections are more than just socializing; they are part of recognizing that your 'tribe' – the group you share a sense of belonging and mutual understanding with – is fundamental to your mental health. Your tribe offers more than companionship; it provides a sense of identity, shared purpose, and most importantly support.

Reflect on your own social connections and consider how these relationships shape your mental well-being. In discovering our tribe, we not only find companionship but also connect to a larger human narrative, deeply rooted in the shared need for connection and belonging.

Community Cure

Psychologist and author Daniel Goleman writes that our relationships with other people act as shock absorbers, cushioning us from the jolts of life.[29] Studies have found that individuals with strong social support recover more quickly from stressful events.[30] Allowing individuals to share burdens and gain different perspectives on their problems can help them access resources and navigate challenging situations.

Indie Gordon told me about one of the communities outside of work that changed everything for her: 'In 2023, I stumbled into a community that completely transformed my life. The funny thing is, I initially resisted joining because it didn't align with my expectations. Little did I know, it was a crucial part of the healing journey I needed at that time and joining turned out to be one of the best decisions of my life.

'In 2023, I received a breast cancer diagnosis, and luckily, it was detected very early. The journey from diagnosis to treatment and healing was lengthy and mentally taxing. As part of my treatment plan, I participated in group counselling with people facing a similar experience. When I joined, the other members were quite different from me, beautiful men and women, considerably older, like in their forties to sixties. At first, I doubted whether I could find value in spending time with people seemingly so different from my normal life. I couldn't have been more wrong.

'I soon realized that this community was exactly where I needed to be. They were filled with wisdom, love and light. Despite the age gap, their stories about the best times of their lives breathed life into me when I was feeling down. Their wealth of life experiences translated into wisdom on various aspects of life, including love, business and professional progression. They became an extension of my family, offering unwavering support in rebuilding my mental health and overall well-being.

'What struck me the most was what they said I gave to them. They mentioned that I brought the ability to see the future. As a glass-half-full person even on my worst days, I inspired them to consider the joy of life post-cancer. It was a beautiful exchange that highlighted the unexpected magic that happens when diverse individuals come together in a community of shared experiences and genuine care.'

There is often an initial resistance towards communities that aren't aligned with your expectations. However, for Indie, this community of members from diverse backgrounds and older age groups unexpectedly became a vital source of wisdom, support and rejuvenation. Their shared experience of battling cancer created a bond that went beyond age and life stages, creating a space where every member could contribute to the collective healing process. Indie's initial doubts about finding value in the group were quickly dispelled as it became a place of hope, love and light, offering perspectives and wisdom that enriched her life through a difficult period.

In turn, Indie's optimism and youthful perspective offered hope and a vision of life beyond illness to the group's older members – showing the mutual benefits of cross-generational community engagement. And Indie's story captures the essence of how non-professional communities can play a crucial role in an individual's healing process – a remedy not just for the physical aspects of a challenge like cancer, but also the mental and emotional tolls.

Research carried out by the University of Michigan has revealed how positive social interactions are closely linked with higher self-esteem.[31] Social interactions provide validation and recognition, reinforcing an individual's sense of worth and identity. The acceptance and understanding you receive from a community can contribute to a healthier self-perception. This reinforcement is not superficial; it is deeply rooted in the psychological make-up of individuals, influencing their day-to-day lives and long-term mental health.

Social groups can motivate individuals to engage in physical activities, maintain a balanced diet, and adhere to other beneficial health practices. Interactions with others play a critical role in shaping our responses to life's challenges and can lead to the development of more adaptive coping mechanisms. Distinguished professor John Cacioppo has observed that our need for social connection is as fundamental as our need for food and water.[32]

I hope you can see now how having a supportive social community outside of work is more than a nicety; it's a necessity for our mental and emotional well-being. And it's not just about the number of friends we have or the social events we attend; the depth and quality of these relationships is what truly matters.

Mac Alonge discussed his personal experiences of trying to build supportive social communities outside of the workplace. 'For me, growing up in the church, I found that community at one point to be very isolating. I grew up attending a fairly rigid and predominantly white church, where whenever you'd ask people how they were they'd reply with an automatic "I'm blessed, how are you". No one really deviated from the social norm of giving the impression that everything was good and there were no issues. My frustrations grew until I met Molly, who was an interesting octogenarian, a little old white lady with no filter. When I asked her how she was, she'd often say things like "I had diarrhoea this morning and I wasn't sure I'd make it to church" – her realness was inspiring. Her honesty meant that you knew exactly how to support her and what she needed, so I decided to copy Molly and I instantly found that my social community became more enriching. What I discovered was the more honest I was with people, the more honest they were with me in return. I've found this has benefited my circle of fellow entrepreneurs. We all realize how tough entrepreneurship can be, but for some reason we all feel the need to put our best foot forward, even if things aren't great.'

Mac's initial sense of isolation in a community where people adhered strictly to social norms of positivity, without space for sharing real struggles or challenges, highlights a common issue found in many social settings. By choosing to emulate Molly's openness, he experienced a transformation in his social interactions, leading to a richer and more supportive community environment. This indicates a fundamental truth about human relationships: authenticity invites authenticity. When individuals choose to share their true experiences, including their vulnerabilities and challenges, it encourages others to do the same. And entrepreneurs, often isolated by the unique challenges of their journey, can benefit immensely from a community where honesty about the difficulties of entrepreneurship is welcomed and shared. Such a community not only provides practical support and advice but also emotional solidarity, reducing feelings of isolation.

Here are a few ways you can be part of social communities outside of work.

I. ENGAGE IN COMMUNITY EVENTS AND ACTIVITIES

Volunteering not only benefits the community but also you. The Corporation for National and Community Service found that 76 per cent of people who volunteered in the last twelve months said that volunteering made them feel healthier.[33] These activities create a sense of collective purpose and identity, crucial for building a supportive social network.

Annisha Taylor spoke about the benefits of volunteering and how it has impacted her sense of identity and self-worth: 'Volunteering as a trustee at the Sutton African and

Caribbean Cultural Organisation (SACCO) has enabled me to provide opportunities for my local community who require more targeted support. My school governor responsibilities enable me to play a vital role in shaping the strategic direction of the school and participate in decision-making processes to improve the quality of experience for pupils and parents. Engaging in volunteer work allows me to see the positive impact I've had on the lives of others, fostering a sense of purpose and fulfilment. Those I volunteer with have similar values and goals, which helps to strengthen our connection for equality and fairness. Both roles have provided opportunities for me to develop my leadership, communication and problem-solving skills, as well as gain valuable experience in governance and management outside of a corporate setting. Most importantly for me, they are fundamental community-engagement roles.'

Volunteering not only contributes positively to the community but also connects you with others. It's a unique way to meet people from diverse backgrounds who are united by a common goal. Whether it's helping at a local shelter, participating in environmental clean-ups or mentoring young people, volunteering offers a sense of purpose and connection. It is an opportunity to give back, but equally to receive – in the form of new friendships and enriched perspectives. Volunteering deepens existing connections and expands your social circle.

2. JOIN INTEREST-BASED GROUPS
AND CULTIVATE A 'SOCIAL HOBBY'

By engaging in activities that you're passionate about, you can connect on a deeper level. The key here is regular participation and active involvement. As psychologist Dr Marisa Franco notes, 'Consistency builds community.'[34] Interest-based groups offer a platform for regular, meaningful interactions, leading to stronger, more supportive social ties. The camaraderie and shared experiences of a social hobby can build lasting bonds, increase happiness and even improve physical health. Imagine the joy of hitting the dance floor for a salsa class or the camaraderie of playing football on a Saturday morning – these experiences can be both exhilarating and nurturing. The key is consistency and inclusivity. This is not just about socializing for the sake of it; it is about creating connections that enrich your life.

Jamelia Donaldson spoke about the Teen Experience, established as personal development workshops for Black and mixed-race girls aged 12–19, and why she found it such an important group to be a part of. 'This non-professional community served as a much-needed reminder of who I once was – a teenage girl navigating the complexities of the world and life. In moments when the gravity and busyness of the professional world threatened to take over, the Teen Experience served as a vital reminder of the "why". It grounded me, reconnecting me with the essence of my journey and the profound influence that meaningful connections within a community can have on personal growth and fulfilment.'

These experiences are crucial for holistic personal growth, as they allow individuals to explore different facets of their identity, acquire new skills, and build relationships based on shared passions rather than professional objectives. And this reconnection to your essence not only enriches your personal life but can also bring a renewed perspective and energy to professional endeavours.

3. CREATE REGULAR MEET-UPS WITH FRIENDS AND ACQUAINTANCES

The *Journal of Social and Personal Relationships* found that it takes about fifty hours of time together to move from acquaintance to casual friend, ninety hours to go from that to simple 'friend', and more than two hundred hours before you can consider someone your close friend.[35] This research highlights the importance of spending time together in nurturing friendships. Have a think. Who are your friends? Is there anyone you want to move from acquaintance to casual friend, or do you want to concentrate more on strengthening your close friendships?

4. SCHEDULE 'SOCIAL MEALS'

Regularly schedule meals with friends, family or colleagues. Research by Oxford University suggests that eating with others boosts our social bonding and feelings of well-being. This practice isn't just about nourishment, it advances connection and opens up conversation. Start transforming your mealtimes into a hub of laughter, stories and shared experiences. Whether it's a dinner out, a picnic in the park, or a regular brunch with friends, these gatherings can be a source of comfort and joy.

Reflect with Raphael

- *Are you creating spaces in your life for shared experiences that not only bring joy but also contribute to your overall well-being?*
- *Reflect on your own social communities outside of work. How have they impacted your sense of identity, self-worth and mental well-being?*
- *Can you think of a time when your social community acted as a 'shock absorber' during a stressful period in your life? How did these interactions help you cope and recover?*

CHAPTER 7

Embracing Diversity and Inclusion within Your Community

Embracing diversity and inclusion goes beyond creating a welcoming environment; it's about utilizing perspectives that drive innovation, understanding and growth.

Analysis by McKinsey & Company reveals that ethnically diverse companies are 35 per cent more likely to outperform their less diverse counterparts.[36] This statistic isn't just a number; it's a testament to the power of varied perspectives when it comes to creativity and problem-solving.

Cecil Peters shared with me his experience of diverse communities: 'I am incredibly fortunate as my team could not be more diverse. However, being diverse is not enough. We also listen to each other's perspectives to learn. That ability to share experiences, empathize, and question without fear has created an invaluable opportunity to learn and grow. I believe I am a better leader through the diverse perspectives I hear.'

The practice of listening to each other's experiences and perspectives with an open mind and empathy is key to an inclusive environment. Cecil believes people become better leaders through engaging with diverse perspectives, and personal growth is not limited to acquiring new knowledge or skills but extends to developing a more empathetic, flexible and inclusive leadership style.

Research published in the *Harvard Business Review* suggests that teams can solve complex problems faster when they are more cognitively diverse.[37] In a community setting, this means that challenges are approached from multiple angles, leading to innovative solutions that might never have emerged in a homogenous group.

Diversity creates tangible benefits for a community, and a report from the Center for Talent Innovation stated that a diverse workforce will also capture a greater share of the consumer market.[38] A diverse group is more likely to understand and cater to a wider array of needs and interests, making the community more relevant and attractive to a broader audience.

But diversity isn't just about problem-solving and out-performing competitors, it's also about the richness it brings to community culture. A community that acknowledges different cultures, languages and traditions becomes a living, breathing celebration of human experience and a more accurate reflection of our society.

Florence Henderson had the opportunity to travel to India, a region that she had been covering for eighteen months in her role as an inclusion leader. 'Our trip coincided with Diwali, the festival of lights, which is celebrated across India – and the world – to mark the triumph of light over darkness. I worked closely with the teams in

India in the run-up to our visit and the sense of excitement was palpable. On arrival in India the offices were decorated in every corner and events included panel discussions, competitions, a fashion show – and of course there was dancing. We were able to experience a major cultural celebration and were honoured to light the Diya lamp and lay flowers at the temple. The employees [at our India office] shared with us the richness of their culture and the differences in the region. That whole trip had a positive impact in demonstrating our commitment to that community.'

By participating in these celebrations and ceremonies, Florence and the leadership team not only showed respect for the local culture but also expressed a genuine commitment to inclusion and diversity, where every culture is valued and celebrated.

Celebrating different cultures goes beyond acknowledgement; it involves immersive experiences that allow individuals to connect with and learn from each other on a more personal level. Such events are great platforms for sharing cultural heritage and stories.

Here are some more key advantages of embedding diversity and inclusion initiatives within your community.

I. ECONOMIC GROWTH AND RESILIENCE

Diversity can be a key driver of economic growth in communities. According to the World Economic Forum, diverse cities tend to be more prosperous. Different cultural backgrounds mean a variety of skills, experiences and networks, which can lead to more dynamic economic activity.

2. IMPROVED DECISION-MAKING AND GOVERNANCE

Diverse communities can benefit from improved decision-making processes. A study by Cloverpop shows that inclusive teams make better business decisions up to 87 per cent of the time.[39] When community decisions involve diverse perspectives, they are more likely to be comprehensive and representative of a community's needs. Speaking with Chris Skeith about the strategies he uses to ensure that community governance structures fairly represent his community, he said the following: 'The community I am privileged to serve boasts a legacy spanning over a century, functioning as a dynamic membership body. While our day-to-day activities reflect a nimble approach, the governance procedures are stipulated in our Memorandum and Articles of Association (M&As), which can only change through proposals and votes at our AGM [annual general meeting] or EGM [extraordinary general meeting].

'Recognizing the need for continual evolution, we embarked on a comprehensive revision of our M&As a few years ago, focusing on the rotation of elected boards. Through thorough research and analysis of our membership, we explored various options to ensure that our board resonated with the diversity within our community.

'In a strategic move, a seemingly simple alteration to limit the term of board members resulted in a more frequent turnover, establishing a cadence that provided opportunities for new members to join each year. This shift developed a diversity of thought within the board, welcoming individuals from varied organizations, sectors, backgrounds and experiences.

'The prospect of altering a system that had seen unwavering dedication from long-standing contributors initially raised concerns. However, the unanimous support for this positive change was a testament to the community's collective commitment to progress.

'This shift not only opened up opportunities but also heightened diversity within the board. These transformative principles are now embedded in our M&As, and we remain steadfast in our commitment to regularly review and adapt them to ensure they stay attuned to the ever-changing times.'

By undertaking a comprehensive revision of its M&As, the community demonstrated a commitment to evolving its governance procedures to reflect its diverse population better. Institutional flexibility and adaptability are important when promoting diversity and inclusion, and in addressing potential resistance and garnering unanimous support for these changes, Chris's community demonstrated a collective commitment to progress and inclusivity, subsequently setting a precedent for embracing positive change even when it challenged long-standing traditions.

Regularly reviewing and adapting governance documents like M&As ensures that these structures remain relevant and responsive to the community's evolving diversity. Such practices not only open up opportunities for broader participation and leadership, but also allow the governance process to benefit from a wide range of insights and experiences, enhancing the community's overall effectiveness.

Chris's community is an inspiring model for other communities and organizations seeking to enhance their governance inclusivity. Through intentional policy changes and a commitment to regular review, communities can create governance environments that truly reflect and benefit from their diversity.

3. SOCIAL COHESION AND EMPATHY

Diversity creates social cohesion and empathy by exposing individuals to different life experiences and viewpoints. Research from the American Psychological Association suggests that diverse environments can reduce prejudices and promote understanding.[40] In a community context, this can lead to a more harmonious and supportive environment.

Reflect with Raphael

- *In what ways can the unique backgrounds of your community members provide unexpected solutions to challenges?*
- *How can the diverse skill sets within your community be harnessed to promote economic development and resilience?*

- *How can you ensure that community governance structures represent diversity, leading to decisions that are more inclusive and beneficial for all?*

Promoting Inclusivity and Breaking Down Barriers

Promoting inclusivity and breaking down barriers in communities is crucial for empowering the whole community. Inclusivity means ensuring that every member, regardless of their background, has equal access to opportunities and resources. It involves actively dismantling barriers – be they cultural, economic or social – that prevent full participation.

This is not just a social or moral endeavour but a strategic one that strengthens the community. Research from Deloitte highlights that inclusive communities are more likely to be prosperous and resilient.[41]

Inclusivity is linked to higher levels of community engagement and satisfaction. A study by the Knight Foundation found that communities with higher levels of inclusion reported stronger attachment and higher community engagement rates.[42] This suggests that when people feel included, they're more likely to contribute positively to their community.

Rebekah Taitt spoke to me about particular times in her life when she felt included, and others when she felt excluded. 'When I was younger, doing gymnastics was a time I felt really included. Me and the other gymnasts shared so many similar goals and experiences which gave us that sense of belonging. We spent a lot of time together, through the good, bad and ugly. I could be at my best or worst and still feel accepted. When I was a younger professional there were times where I felt excluded, and sometimes I feel in a true professional community I am not always included. For me, it gives me a fire in my belly to break glass ceilings or the status quo and create my own communities where everyone is embraced.'

Inclusion – and the lack thereof – can have a huge impact within various communities, from sports to professional environments. Rebekah's story during her time as a gymnast highlights the positive effects of shared goals and activities in creating a supportive community. Her early experience of acceptance, regardless of performance, indicates the confidence inclusion can create in individuals.

Contrasting these positive memories, Rebekah's description of feeling excluded in her professional life sheds light on the challenges of exclusion in work environments. Feelings of being left out can significantly impact your sense of belonging. But Rebekah has taken this negativity and turned it into something positive, leading to a drive to challenge and change the status quo. Her resolve to 'break glass ceilings' and create inclusive communities where everyone is embraced is a proactive response to personal experiences of exclusion.

Opeyemi Sofoluke also spoke about proactively engaging with diversity and inclusion groups and initiatives to strengthen communities. As the Diversity, Equity and Inclusion Leader at one of the biggest tech companies in the world, she had the following insights to share: 'Through-out my career, I've witnessed the transformative impact of well-structured Employee Resource Groups (ERGs). These are internal communities for employees with shared identities. ERGs, when supported by strategic planning, sponsorship and adequate budget allocation, can be a key vehicle for driving engagement and belonging.

'An intriguing observation I have made across various organizations, however, is the potential absence of community within these groups when there's a lack of diversity among their members. This underscores the personal nature of community, where individuals may feel disconnected despite outwardly appearing to be part of a group designed for them. In my experience with ERGs, especially women's groups, the leadership team of these groups in corporate settings was often predominantly composed of white women. This dynamic posed challenges for me – and, I imagine, other ethnic minority women who may find that some of the concerns we encounter in the workplace differ from the majority of the group's experiences and concerns.

'Early in my career, I actively participated in a number of ERGs, including the women's groups, seeking to build connections and broaden my understanding of various areas within the organization. While these groups offered informative sessions on career development, I experienced discomfort during the networking part of these events, sensing a lack of genuine interest in my contributions. This prompted me to withdraw from these settings, ultimately finding a more resonant community within the Black network and eventually assuming a leadership role.

'Reflecting on these experiences, diversity and inclusion are significant factors in fostering community. However, it is crucial that these spaces acknowledge and embrace the intersectionalities within the group to cultivate deeper and more meaningful connections, avoiding the formation of cliques within the community.'

Here Opeyemi sheds light on the nuanced complexities of inclusivity within ERGs, and the broader implications for creating genuinely inclusive communities in the workplace. ERGs are designed to be supportive spaces for employees sharing similar identities or experiences, aiming to promote engagement, belonging and diversity. However, the effectiveness of these groups often hinges on their ability to recognize and celebrate the diversity within their own ranks.

When the leadership does not reflect the full spectrum of identities and experiences within the group, this can inadvertently marginalize members who do not see their concerns and challenges adequately represented. This can lead to feelings of disconnection and exclusion – the very issues ERGs are meant to address.

Opeyemi's personal experience of feeling discomfort and a lack of genuine interest in her contributions from others during ERG events is a poignant reminder of the work still needed to break down barriers within these supposed safe spaces. It illustrates the importance of not just forming these groups but actively working to ensure they are welcoming and inclusive to all members, regardless of background or identity.

By drawing from personal experiences of both inclusion and exclusion, individuals can become ambassadors for change, advocating for environments that recognize and celebrate differences.

Promoting inclusivity and breaking down barriers is not just about fairness; it's about creating a community where everyone thrives. But this requires intentional actions and strategies. Each community is unique, so it's important to tailor these approaches to fit specific or local needs and contexts. By implementing some of the strategies below, communities can work towards becoming more inclusive, equitable and harmonious places, where every member feels valued and empowered.

1. OPEN DIALOGUE AND EDUCATION

Creating platforms for open, honest dialogue is crucial in promoting understanding among diverse community members. Educational programmes and workshops that focus on cultural awareness, anti-bias training and the importance of diversity can be instrumental. This approach encourages individuals to acknowledge and respect differences, ultimately leading to a more inclusive environment.

2. ENSURING EQUITABLE ACCESS TO COMMUNITY RESOURCES

Inclusivity is about providing equal opportunities for all; this can be achieved by ensuring that community resources, such as public spaces and education, are accessible to everyone, regardless of their background. This might require language translation services, disability accommodations, or targeted outreach programmes to underserved groups.

3. INCLUSIVE DECISION-MAKING PROCESSES

Inclusion in decision-making processes ensures that the diverse voices within a community are not just heard but are influential in shaping policies and initiatives. This could involve forming diverse advisory committees, conducting community surveys, and holding town hall meetings where everyone can contribute. By involving diverse community members in decision-making, policies are more likely to be equitable and representative. Ask yourself how the decision-making processes in your community can be adjusted to represent its diverse population better.

4. DIVERSE HIRING PRACTICES

If you are going to create a diverse and inclusive organization, you must get your hiring practices right. It's imperative you implement hiring practices that actively seek out candidates from a variety of backgrounds, experiences and perspectives.

This can include partnering with diverse recruitment agencies, posting job ads in diverse communities, and ensuring that job descriptions are inclusive and non-biased. The impact of this approach will enable a more diverse workforce, bringing a wealth of different perspectives to the company.

5. INCLUSIVE LEADERSHIP TRAINING
AND POLICY DEVELOPMENT

It all starts from the top; you must ensure that those who are in key decision-making roles are practising inclusive leadership, and you need to be able to provide them with the relevant training. This training should cover understanding unconscious bias, allyship, diverse recruitment, effective communication across diverse teams, and strategies for creating an inclusive environment.

The impact of this is a leadership team that is equipped to nurture a diverse workforce, leading to increased employee engagement and satisfaction. According to Deloitte, inclusive leaders can help boost team performance by up to 17 per cent and decision-making quality by 20 per cent.[43]

Involve a diverse group of employees in developing company policies to ensure that they are inclusive and consider the needs of all employees. This approach ensures that policies are not just top–down directives but are shaped by the experiences of all those they impact.

6. EMPLOYEE RESOURCE GROUPS (ERGS)

Any company without an Employee Resource Group is falling behind. If you are an employee, look for opportunities to join ones that resonate with you; and encourage and support the formation of ERGs if they don't yet exist.

ERGs are employee-led and focus on specific demographic groups, providing support, advocacy and professional development opportunities. They can have an incredible impact by empowering employees and encouraging a sense of belonging among all members of the workforce.

7. CELEBRATING DIVERSITY THROUGH COMMUNITY EVENTS AND INITIATIVES

Organizing events and initiatives that celebrate the diverse cultures, traditions and backgrounds of community members can unite your community and help build respect. These could be anything that highlights different community members' experiences and stories. Such events not only educate but also build bridges of understanding.

'Cultural events, particularly festivals, are great ways to celebrate diversity,' Mike Sealy told me. 'The Notting Hill Carnival in the UK is a great example of bringing diverse communities together for fun, laughter, dancing and general socializing. It has been running every year since the mid-1960s and initially as a response to developing race relations and easing the intercultural tensions at that time by celebrating Caribbean culture through lively music and colourful costumes. Today it is an integral part of London's diverse community and landscape.'

The Notting Hill Carnival stands as a testament to the power of cultural events in promoting diversity and inclusion within a community. Originating as a response to racial tensions, this annual event has gone far beyond its initial purpose, evolving into a celebration that encapsulates the richness of London's multicultural landscape. By showcasing Caribbean culture through its lively music, dance and colourful costumes, the carnival not only honours the traditions of one community but also invites a broader audience to partake in and appreciate this cultural heritage.

The significance of these events extends beyond entertainment; they serve as crucial platforms for dialogue, understanding and unity across different populations. By embracing and celebrating the diversity of London's residents, the Notting Hill Carnival exemplifies how multiculturalism can be a source of strength and vibrancy. It is a model for other cities and communities that are aiming to celebrate and integrate their own diverse populations.

Rebekah Taitt spoke about a programme that she found effective in promoting an understanding of diversity and inclusion within communities. 'The best experience I've had has been reverse mentoring or two-way mentoring. These programmes help you build a relationship with someone which allows you both to relate to each other. Two-way mentoring helps me on a day-to-day basis. It gives me professional support and my relationship with fellow professionals of other races has helped to educate them on D&I. They now "see" people like me, which maybe they didn't before.'

This approach to mentoring dismantles traditional hierarchies and knowledge flows, creating a space where both parties can learn from each other. By facilitating relationships between individuals of differing backgrounds, experiences and levels of expertise, two-way mentoring embodies the embracing of diversity within a community. It not only provides professional support but also serves as an educational bridge, enhancing awareness and understanding of diversity and inclusion issues among its participants.

This method of mentoring is particularly effective in celebrating diversity, as it encourages direct, personal interactions that challenge preconceptions and encourage a deeper understanding of the unique challenges and perspectives of diverse individuals. Through these relationships, mentors/mentees are exposed to new viewpoints and life experiences, which can significantly alter their perceptions and attitudes. Individuals who may not have previously recognized the importance of D&I initiatives can gain first-hand insight into the experiences of those from underrepresented groups, leading to a more inclusive mindset and behaviours that support diversity. Two-way mentoring contributes to a culture of inclusivity by demonstrating that everyone, regardless of their position or background, has valuable insights and experiences to share.

Reflect with Raphael

- *Consider the impact of a truly inclusive community: how would breaking down these barriers change the day-to-day experiences of its members?*
- *What untapped potential lies in the segments of your community that currently feel marginalized or underrepresented?*
- *Think about the barriers that exist in your own community. How can they be dismantled? What steps can be taken to ensure that every voice is heard?*

- *What kinds of events could be organized in your community to celebrate its diversity and promote inclusivity?*

Celebrating Differences

Embracing and celebrating diversity is about actively recognizing and valuing the unique contributions of everyone. This approach is not just socially beneficial but also vital for communal innovation and cohesion. Consider how powerful it is to have a community where every cultural story, personal background and distinct viewpoint enriches the collective narrative.

The celebration of diversity also has implications for community resilience and problem-solving. Research from diverse fields suggests that when a variety of perspectives are integrated, communities become more adaptable and innovative. This concept extends beyond the realm of creativity; it encompasses the ability to respond to challenges and changes more effectively. A community that embraces varied cultural wisdoms and experiences may find unique and sustainable solutions to environmental or social challenges.

Hosting events that showcase the diverse cultures within a community is a powerful way to celebrate differences. Such events not only provide a platform for different cultural groups to share their heritage but also offer an opportunity for others to learn about and appreciate these differences.

Studies in social psychology suggest that when individuals feel valued and recognized for their unique identities, there is a marked improvement in mental health and overall life satisfaction.[44] This then has a ripple effect, enhancing community solidarity.

Celebrating differences is about creating a community where diversity is not just a backdrop but a central, active part of the community's identity and strength. It's about shaping a community in which each person's story contributes to a larger, more vibrant and resilient narrative.

Reflect with Raphael

- *What new approaches and solutions might emerge from a richly diverse community?*
- *What unique cultural aspects exist within your community, and how can they be highlighted and celebrated in a way that brings people together?*
- *What steps can be taken to identify and eliminate barriers to accessing community resources?*

CHAPTER 8

Community Leadership: Guiding and Inspiring Your Tribe

'Leaders don't create followers, they create more leaders.'

– Tom Peters

Community leadership plays a crucial role in the foundation and maintenance of a dynamic community. A skilled community leader is more than just an organizer or manager; they are a source of inspiration and empowerment for their community members.

A study in the *Harvard Business Review* says that effective community leadership can enhance member engagement by up to 50 per cent.[45] This is particularly important because communities with high engagement levels are known to be more resilient, innovative and supportive environments.

Guiding and inspiring your tribe is an integral part of leadership. Simon Sinek famously said, 'Leadership is not about being in charge. It's about taking care of those in your charge.'[46] It is the leader's responsibility to charge and inspire their community members. This position must not be taken lightly, and if done correctly it can yield exciting results.

The balance between guiding and empowering is a delicate one, and as a leader you must navigate the fine line of providing direction and also allowing space for members to express themselves and grow independently. As a father of three, this reminds me of my kids. Yes, it's important for me to guide them, but equally it's important to give them space to develop within the boundaries of our household values.

The Center for Creative Leadership suggests that leaders who exhibit empathetic leadership and promote diversity of thought are more successful in developing strong, inclusive communities.[47] This approach is increasingly important in a world that is often polarized and fragmented.

Lynsey Campbell's trust-first approach highlights this. 'It's all about radical trust or a trust-first environment as a leader,' she told me. 'All too often leaders feel that others have to earn trust. I completely disagree. Trust-first is such an incredible way to empower and enable others from the start – generating ideas and being open to mistakes and learning fast from them.'

The concept of 'radical trust' or a 'trust-first' environment diverges from the conventional wisdom. But by adopting a trust-first attitude, leaders set a foundation of empowerment, signalling to members that their contributions are valued and that they are supported in their endeavours, even when they make mistakes.

The emphasis on being open to mistakes and quickly learning from them is a key element of creating a culture where members feel safe to experiment, take risks and explore new ideas. This kind of environment not only accelerates personal and group learning but also promotes a sense of ownership and accountability among community members. When leaders demonstrate trust in the abilities and judgement of their members, it encourages a more engaged, proactive community dynamic.

Leaders who adopt a trust-first approach act as facilitators and supporters of their community members' growth and exploration. This shift requires a level of humility and a willingness to embrace uncertainty, recognizing that the path to innovation and growth often involves navigating failures and setbacks.

Cecil Peters encourages his team members to outline the problem for themselves, so that in articulating it 'they can start to think about the root causes and then what needs to change to deal with the cause of the issue rather than the symptoms. As a leader sometimes we have to speak less and trust our community to find their path. Only if they are truly stuck would I perhaps offer direction. Similarly, it is important to create safe zones such that members can try out different areas without fear or ridicule.'

This method of leadership puts importance on self-discovery and independent growth within the community, reinforcing the idea that effective leaders serve more as facilitators of learning rather than dictators of action.

Creating 'safe zones' so members can experiment and explore different solutions without fear of ridicule or failure is a key strategy. This approach not only encourages members to stretch their capabilities and try new things, it also builds a stronger community where support and constructive feedback are the norm.

The practice of speaking less and trusting the community to find its path represents a significant shift from traditional leadership models. It suggests a confidence in the wisdom and capabilities of the community members, allowing them to navigate on their own journeys. This empowerment in turn leads to more engaged and motivated members who feel valued and understood.

Mastering the art of balancing guidance with empowerment involves knowing when to step in with direction and when to step back to allow for independent problem-solving. It also requires the creation of an inclusive and supportive environment where experimentation is encouraged and failures are seen as stepping stones to success.

By encouraging problem articulation, creating safe zones for experimentation and trusting members to navigate challenges, community leaders can facilitate meaningful growth and development.

Transitioning from Community Member to Leader

Transitioning from a community member to a leader represents a significant shift in role and responsibility, and marks a critical phase in the life of the community as a whole.

Transformation is not just about acquiring a title; it involves a change in perspective and function. One study has revealed that individuals who transition into leadership roles experience a 70 per cent increase in their ability to influence community initiatives positively.[48] Assuming such a role within a community gives you immense power. As a leader you should also be nurturing those you lead, as the next leader is likely to come from within your community.

The journey from member to leader is characterized by a deepening understanding of the community's needs, aspirations and dynamics. John Quincy Adams said that, 'If your actions inspire others to dream more, learn more, do more and become more, you are a leader.'[49] This is the essence of the transition – it's about evolving into someone who not only participates in but also sets the direction and tone for a community's future. To become a leader, you need to become someone who inspires others to dream and do more.

So how do you do that? To navigate the transition successfully, you must understand what challenges this transition presents in terms of maintaining relationships and gaining respect. Research suggests that new leaders who maintain their authenticity and continue to engage in active listening are more successful in gaining the trust and support of their community members.[50]

As a leader you must be wary of how your position impacts relationships within the community; you will have to make tough decisions while remaining approachable and empathetic to your community members' perspectives.

There are several strategies you can employ to ensure that your transition into leadership is smooth and you continue to create unity and cooperation within the community.

I. DEVELOP STRONG COMMUNICATION SKILLS

Communication is key to effective leadership. The American Management Association found that leaders who excel in communication are 50 per cent more likely to manage and lead their communities successfully.[51] Effective communication involves not just conveying messages but also listening and engaging in meaningful dialogues. George Bernard Shaw famously said, 'The single biggest problem in communication is the illusion that it has taken place.'[52] You need to ensure that your communication is not just heard but understood and acted upon.

2. CULTIVATE EMOTIONAL INTELLIGENCE (EQ)

EQ is critical in leadership. According to the Harvard Business School, leaders with high emotional intelligence are more likely to create an environment of trust and collaboration.[53] Emotional intelligence involves self-awareness and the ability to manage your own emotions and those of others. Daniel Goleman, an American psychologist, says that, 'Emotional intelligence does not mean merely "being nice". At strategic moments it may demand not "being nice", but rather, for example, bluntly confronting someone with an uncomfortable but consequential truth they've been avoiding.'[54] Transitioning leaders need to develop and use their EQ to navigate the complexities of community dynamics. You need to be prepared to be nice, but also 'not nice' when it is required.

3. BUILD TRUST THROUGH AUTHENTICITY AND INTEGRITY

Trust is the foundation for any strong leader. Generally, leaders who display high levels of integrity are more likely to gain and retain the trust of their community members. Authenticity in leadership means being true to your values and beliefs while being open to others' ideas and feedback. New leaders need to balance staying true to their values with the need to adapt to their new role.

4. LEAD BY EXAMPLE

Leading by example is perhaps the most powerful tool a leader has. One paper on leadership development in business schools found that leaders who 'walk the talk' are far more effective in motivating their team.[55] Polymath Albert Schweitzer said, 'Example is not the main thing in influencing others, it is the only thing.' You need to ensure your actions reflect your words and beliefs, thereby inspiring others to follow your lead.

Reflect with Raphael

- *How can your leadership style and approach impact your engagement within the community?*

- *If you have transitioned from being a community member to a leader, what were the biggest challenges you faced in this shift? How did you overcome them, and what did you learn in the process?*
- *How do you think emotional intelligence (EQ) plays a role in effective community leadership? Can you think of a scenario where a leader's EQ significantly influenced a community's dynamics?*
- *In your opinion, what are the key strategies a leader can use to build trust and demonstrate authenticity within a community?*
- *Think of a leader who has inspired you. What qualities or actions made them inspiring, and how did they influence your personal or professional growth?*

Leadership Skills: How to Inspire and Motivate Your Community

Developing leadership skills is a critical component of guiding and inspiring a community effectively. This development goes beyond management tactics; it encompasses having a vision, inspiring trust, and motivating members to achieve their collective goals.

According to a study by the Center for Leadership Development, communities led by individuals with advanced leadership skills show a 60 per cent higher rate of active engagement and success in their initiatives.[56] There is a direct correlation between leadership skills and a community's effectiveness.

But what makes a leader truly inspiring? It is their ability to articulate a vision, and their capacity to connect on a personal level. The *Harvard Business Review* indicates that leaders who combine strategic vision with personal compassion see higher levels of loyalty and motivation among their community members.[57] It's this blend of skills that makes individuals feel valued and part of a larger purpose.

The development of leadership skills is an ongoing process. It involves continuous learning, self-reflection and adaptation. In developing these skills, you must also consider the diverse nature of your community.

Here are some of the key leadership skills and attributes you need to continue to develop to inspire and motivate your community.

I. CONTINUOUS LEARNING AND SELF-IMPROVEMENT

Effective leaders are perpetual learners. A McKinsey report states that leaders who engage in continuous learning are 2.5 times more effective in achieving their goals.[58] This involves staying informed about new trends, understanding the evolving needs of the community, and being open to feedback. As Mahatma Gandhi famously said, 'Live as if you were to die tomorrow. Learn as if you were to live for ever.' As a leader, think about how you can integrate continuous learning into your daily routine, and how you can translate this into actionable improvements within your community.

2. VISION-SETTING AND GOAL ALIGNMENT

A leader must be adept at setting a clear, compelling vision and aligning community goals with this vision. According to a study by Bain & Company, organizations led by vision-driven leaders are twice as likely to achieve above-median financial performance.[59] Articulating a vision can significantly boost engagement and motivation. You must craft a vision that not only aligns with the community's objectives but also ignites passion and enthusiasm.

3. RESILIENCE AND ADAPTABILITY

In today's rapidly changing world, a leader's ability to be resilient and adaptable is paramount. Research has shown that adaptable leaders are 6.7 times more likely to be successful.[60] Resilience helps leaders navigate challenges and setbacks, maintaining a steady course for the community amidst turbulence. Leaders must show resilience within themselves and their communities, and this resilience will translate into sustained motivation and progress.

4. EMPOWERING AND DEVELOPING OTHERS

True leadership involves empowering others to take the initiative and develop their own leadership qualities. When leaders delegate responsibilities and encourage others to take on leadership roles, community members develop a sense of ownership and accountability.

Reflect with Raphael

- *What resources and practices can you employ to continuously evolve your leadership style to meet the changing needs of your community?*
- *How can you ensure that your leadership approach is inclusive and resonates with a varied audience?*
- *Furthermore, how can you maintain your authenticity while adapting your style to suit different situations and challenges?*
- *What strategies can leaders employ to empower their community members, and how does this empowerment contribute to building a more dynamic and motivated community?*

Responsibilities of Community Leadership

Responsibilities of community leadership extend far beyond administrative duties; they encompass the development and welfare of the community.

Effective community leaders bear the weight of various roles: visionary, facilitator, mediator and mentor. Leaders who actively engage in these multifaceted roles can significantly increase community participation. A leader can be instrumental to the vibrancy and cohesion of their community. A great community leader is adaptable, so think about your skills and how you can use these attributes to benefit your community.

Leaders have the responsibility to mediate conflicts and facilitate constructive dialogues. Conflict resolution does not only require diplomacy but also empathy and fairness; alongside this, a leader must mentor and empower others, cultivating future leaders. All these responsibilities are crucial for the sustainable development of a community.

These responsibilities highlight the nature of community leadership. It's about guiding a community towards a shared vision, maintaining inclusivity, resolving conflicts and empowering members, all while maintaining the delicate balance between leading and serving.

Reflect with Raphael

- *How can you navigate conflicts to maintain harmony and mutual respect within your community?*
- *What approaches can you take to mentor and empower community members?*
- *How can you communicate your vision effectively to ensure it aligns with and motivates the community?*
- *What strategies can you implement to mentor and empower your community members effectively, creating a culture of shared leadership and responsibility?*
- *How can you navigate conflicts constructively and transform these challenges into opportunities for growth and understanding?*

Inspiring Others to Contribute and Engage

This aspect of leadership is about igniting and motivating others to participate and invest actively in your community. It's a critical element for the health and vitality of any community.

Simon Sinek has said that, 'People don't buy what you do; they buy why you do it. And what you do simply proves what you believe.'[61] Inspiring leadership is rooted in a leader's ability to convey a compelling 'why' that connects deeply with community members, aligning with their values and aspirations.

Inspiring others involves recognizing and appreciating their contributions. William James, a famous American philosopher, once wrote, 'The deepest principle in human nature is the craving to be appreciated.' Leaders need to effectively acknowledge and celebrate the efforts of community members in order to develop a culture of appreciation and motivation.

Storytelling is another key way to inspire engagement. Stories have the power to connect people, evoke emotions and drive action. Using storytelling as a tool to communicate your vision, share successes and highlight the impact of community engagement will go a long way.

Now think about your community. How can you create opportunities for members to contribute in meaningful ways? This involves understanding the diverse skills and interests within the community and providing platforms where these can be utilized effectively.

Here are some of the key ways you can inspire others to contribute and engage with your community.

1. ARTICULATE A COMPELLING VISION

A clearly defined and compelling vision can be a powerful motivator for community members. It's essential for leaders to articulate a vision that is both aspirational and relatable – one that members can see themselves being a part of and which aligns with the values and goals of the community.

2. RECOGNIZE AND VALUE CONTRIBUTIONS

People are more likely to engage when they feel their contributions are recognized and valued. Acknowledging the efforts and achievements of community members, whether big or small, shows appreciation and encourages continued participation. Research by Deloitte has revealed that recognition is a key factor in employee happiness, which can be extrapolated to community settings.[62]

3. A SENSE OF INCLUSION

Creating an environment where members feel included in a larger community is crucial for engagement. This involves building strong relationships, promoting inclusivity and encouraging open communication.

4. EMPOWERMENT THROUGH OPPORTUNITIES AND RESOURCES

Providing opportunities for members to contribute in meaningful ways and equipping them with the necessary resources can greatly enhance engagement. This could involve offering training, workshops or platforms for members to enable them to showcase their skills and ideas.

Reflect with Raphael

- *What strategies can you employ to identify the unique talents within your community, and ensure that each member feels valued and empowered to contribute?*
- *How can you craft and communicate a vision that not only drives action but also resonates with the deeper aspirations of your community members?*
- *How can you create a recognition system that genuinely appreciates contributions and encourages others to step forward?*

CHAPTER 9

Community in a Digital Age: Leveraging Social Media and Technology

Integrating social media and technology into community-building is paramount. The expansive reach of online platforms has revolutionized the concept of community, creating a new era of global connectivity. The digital landscape offers myriad opportunities for communities to grow, interact and evolve in ways that were once unimaginable. It enables quick and widespread dissemination of information, facilitates real-time communication, and provides platforms for problem-solving.

Digital analyst Brian Solis encapsulated this evolution when he said, 'Social media is about sociology and psychology more than technology.' Communities can leverage digital tools to create genuine human connections that go beyond the often-superficial interactions on these platforms.

The global nature of digital communities allows for the aggregation of diverse perspectives, enriching the community experience with a multitude of voices and ideas.

This diversity, however, also brings forth the challenge of creating a cohesive and engaging community experience.

There's also the critical aspect of inclusivity in these digital spaces. As communities increasingly rely on digital platforms, issues of digital literacy and access become more prominent. This digital divide can create barriers to participation, potentially excluding certain segments of the community. Leaders must ensure they can bridge the divide to ensure equitable access and participation for all community members.

Kanya King spoke about the opportunities and challenges the digital age has offered her business. 'We've embraced social media and online platforms for direct communication with our audience, hosting live streaming events and Q&A sessions. The shift towards digital music distribution has allowed us to reach a larger audience, especially independent artists. Collaborating with platforms like TikTok for music distribution has been a key strategy, ensuring we adapt to consumer behaviour and how music is consumed digitally.'

Live streaming events and Q&A sessions are innovative approaches to creating real-time, interactive experiences that deepen the connection between an artist and their fan base, making the community experience more accessible and engaging. And the shift towards digital music distribution is a significant change in how music is shared and discovered. In many ways this evolution has democratized access to music, enabling independent artists to reach wider audiences without the traditional barriers posed by physical distribution channels. The success of partnerships with platforms like TikTok shows the importance of aligning with current consumer behaviours and preferences for digital content consumption. TikTok, with its vast, diverse user base and unique content format, offers artists a dynamic space in which to share music, engage with listeners, and tap into new fan communities through viral trends and challenges.

Technology and social media are critical when it comes to adapting to and shaping the digital landscape of music consumption and community engagement. By leveraging these digital tools, artists and music industry professionals can develop a more inclusive, expansive and interactive community, spreading beyond geographical boundaries and creating opportunities for innovation and growth.

The digital age has undeniably transformed the dynamics of community-building. Social media and technology are not just tools for connectivity; they represent a fundamental shift in how communities form, operate and thrive. They have the potential to bring people together for collective action, learning and support in unprecedented ways.

Reflect with Raphael

- *How can you create a sense of intimacy and authenticity in a digital space that often feels vast and impersonal?*
- *In what ways can you bridge this divide to ensure equitable access and participation for all community members?*

Harnessing the Power of Online
Communities and Social Media

According to a report by GWI, an average person spends more than two hours on social media platforms daily,[63] and the Pew Research Center says nearly two-thirds of social media users are engaged in activism on these platforms.[64] These statistics show the extensive influence these platforms have on our lives.

Using these platforms is about tapping into this vast potential of connection. 'Social media creates communities, not markets,' as marketing consultant Don Schultz said. This perspective shifts the focus from using digital platforms as marketing tools to recognizing them as spaces for community-building and finding your tribe.

Online communities provide a unique opportunity for crowd-sourcing ideas, knowledge, and support. Platforms like Instagram, X (Twitter), LinkedIn and specialized forums enable people to come together over shared interests or challenges. They are powerful tools for advocacy and social change, and give a voice to the voiceless. It's beautiful to see that we have platforms with the potential to mobilize large groups of people for a cause.

I spoke with Marvyn Harrison, founder of Dope Black Dads, about why he built his community and the importance of social media in its growth. Marvyn is a visionary leader who is renowned for his ability to deliver business goals and drive cultural change through sound strategy, communication and people management.

'I launched my own community in 2018, when I was curious about the experience other Black men were having during fatherhood,' he said. 'Dope Black Dads expanded into multiple countries and helped thousands of people through our podcast and social media storytelling. Dope Black Dads leverages digital platforms to enhance communication. Social media, messaging apps and video conferencing tools are vital in connecting our community across the world.'

Another individual focusing on supporting men via digital platforms is Sayce Holmes-Lewis, founder of Mentivity, an alternative education provision and mentoring organization that offers aspirational support to young people, families, schools and caregivers. Sayce utilizes the power of online communities and digital platforms to create change by supporting young people to realize their optimum potential without the need to code-switch or erase the cultural identities that uniquely connect them through culture, estates, boroughs and postcodes.

As beautiful as it is, the digital age also brings challenges in the form of information overload, misinformation and the increased difficulty of maintaining genuine connections. Leaders of online communities must navigate these challenges carefully.

Here are some key ways we can harness the power of online communities and social media.

I. CREATE ENGAGING AND RELEVANT CONTENT

Create content that is engaging, informative and relevant to the interests of the community. According to a study by HubSpot, content that resonates with its audience's interests and needs increases engagement by up to 50 per cent.[65] The challenge for community leaders is to understand their audience deeply and provide relevant content that will keep them engaged. Joel Beya is the founder of a successful sports platform in the UK called CheekySport, as well as a prominent content creator and the co-presenter of a podcast alongside Manchester United legend Rio Ferdinand. He told me that when it comes to creating engaging and relevant content as a digital content manager for a football podcast, where resonant content often includes match analysis, player interviews and behind-the-scenes insights, 'customizing content to align with current events, transfer news and fan opinions enhances relevance. To stimulate interaction I employ social media polls, live Q&A sessions and listener feedback segments. It's also important to establish an online platform dedicated to community discussions, along with interactive elements like quizzes or challenges; this promotes engagement. Regularly acknowledging and integrating audience input into the podcast creates a positive atmosphere, strengthening the connection between the content and my audience.'

Joel's podcast exemplifies a collaborative approach to content creation. It's a strategy that not only validates the contributions of its audience but also strengthens the connection between content and consumer. By treating the audience as co-creators, Joel inspires a sense of ownership and investment among the podcast's listeners, which can lead to increased loyalty and engagement over time. This approach not only enhances the quality and relevance of the content, it also promotes a strong sense of connection among the audience, leading to sustained engagement and growth.

2. FACILITATE MEANINGFUL INTERACTIONS

Social media isn't just about broadcasting messages; it's two-way communication. Facebook groups, Instagram Lives, X (Twitter) Room chats and LinkedIn forums provide opportunities for discussions, Q&A sessions, and more. This interactive approach can strengthen a sense of community.

3. UTILIZE ANALYTICS AND FEEDBACK FOR IMPROVEMENT

Utilize analytics tools that provide insights into user engagement and content performance on social media platforms. Analyse this data and you'll understand what matters to your audience so you can refine your strategies accordingly. Soliciting direct feedback from community members can be invaluable.

4. PROMOTE COLLABORATION AND COMMUNITY-DRIVEN INITIATIVES

Empowering community members to contribute content, share their expertise and/or lead discussions can be highly effective. This approach not only diversifies the content but also gives members a sense of ownership and investment in the community. Adobe's 2019 Brand Content Survey found that user-generated content increases engagement and trust among community members.[66]

Reflect with Raphael

- *How can you leverage online platforms to cultivate meaningful interactions and strong community bonds?*
- *How can you harness your community to drive positive social change and bring attention to important issues?*
- *How can you ensure your community remains authentic and a valuable space for members?*
- *Find out what topics your community are passionate about. What information do they find valuable? And how can content be crafted to not only attract attention but also encourage interaction and discussion?*
- *How can you encourage and facilitate community-driven initiatives, turning passive followers into active contributors?*

The Benefits and Drawbacks of Virtual Interaction

Being aware of the benefits and drawbacks of virtual interaction is crucial for a comprehensive understanding of how social media and technology impact our communities.

Benefits of Virtual Interaction

I. GLOBAL CONNECTIVITY

One of the most significant benefits of virtual interaction is the ability to connect with people worldwide. Global reach breaks down geographical barriers, enabling the exchange of ideas and cultures across the world. According to a report by Statista, there are over 4.2 billion active social media users globally,[67] highlighting the extensive network that virtual platforms offer.

2. ACCESSIBILITY AND INCLUSIVITY

Virtual interactions provide accessibility to individuals who may be limited by physical, geographical or social constraints. People with disabilities or those living in remote areas, for instance, can participate in online communities, making these platforms both inclusive and diverse.

3. FLEXIBILITY AND CONVENIENCE

The convenience of engaging with others at any time and place is a notable benefit of virtual interactions. This flexibility allows for more frequent and diverse forms of communication, accommodating various lifestyles and schedules.

4. RESOURCES FOR LEARNING

Virtual platforms serve as valuable resources for learning and teamwork. They facilitate knowledge-sharing and collective problem-solving, often leading to innovation and growth.

Drawbacks of Virtual Interaction

1. LACK OF PHYSICAL CUES AND A PERSONAL TOUCH

Virtual interaction often lacks the nuances of face-to-face communication, such as body language and tone, which can lead to misunderstandings. Albert Mehrabian, a professor of psychology, stated that 93 per cent of communication effectiveness is determined by non-verbal cues,[68] which indicates the limitations of digital communication.

2. RISK OF MISINFORMATION AND ECHO CHAMBERS

The spread of misinformation is a significant concern in virtual spaces. Additionally, social media algorithms can create echo chambers, reinforcing users' existing beliefs and limiting exposure to diverse perspectives. This can lead to polarization and misinformation.

3. DIGITAL DIVIDE AND ACCESSIBILITY ISSUES

Despite the inclusivity of online platforms, the digital divide remains a challenge. Access to technology and digital literacy skills are not universal, potentially excluding segments of the population from virtual communities.

Mike Sealy shared further thoughts with me on the digital divide: 'The biggest challenge with digital technology is that it is continually being updated and improved and it can be very difficult to keep pace. The digital divide is a very thin line where one minute you can be very competent and the next you can struggle and fall behind. There needs to be training and education delivered in a simple and easy to understand format. Community networks can play a key role by having somewhere where the community can access the internet, especially for those who may not have personal broadband access, or for those who want to learn from scratch or improve their basic knowledge to a higher level of competency. I believe that local libraries, community centres and even schools provide this service, but the community can play a big part in encouraging participation.'

Addressing this challenge requires innovative approaches that prioritize simplicity, accessibility and community support.

Training and education are fundamental to bridging the digital divide, particularly when delivered in formats that are easily understandable and accessible to all. Simplifying complex technological concepts and providing step-by-step guides can demystify digital tools and platforms, making them more approachable for individuals who might feel overwhelmed by the rapid changes in technology.

The community itself plays a crucial role in encouraging participation and creating a supportive environment for digital learning. Community-led initiatives, peer mentoring programmes and digital literacy campaigns can motivate individuals to engage with digital technologies and participate in digital communities.

4. IMPACT ON MENTAL HEALTH

Excessive use of digital platforms can negatively impact mental health. Various studies, including ones from the American Psychological Association, have shown correlations between heavy social media use and increased feelings of loneliness, anxiety and depression.[69]

Balancing Online and Offline Community Engagement

A healthy equilibrium is essential for a well-rounded community experience that leverages the expansive reach of technology while preserving the intrinsic value of in-person interactions. In today's digitally dominated world, the ease and immediacy of online engagement is undeniable. Yet the richness of offline interactions, where nuances and emotions are more readily perceived and shared, cannot be overlooked.

Community activity needs to be structured to incorporate both online and offline elements, thereby enriching the overall community. I spoke with Elizabeth Uviebinené about how in an increasingly digital world she balances online and offline community engagement.

'I'm still balancing offline and online networking,' she said. 'I really look at networking as an opportunity to build relationships with people. It's about finding common ground, interests and shared values. This could be following someone I admire online, commenting on their posts to show support, etc. I also balance things out by reaching out to them, arranging coffee, and genuinely being curious about who they are, what they're about and, ultimately, how I can add value. I think nothing beats in-person networking because people buy into people, you can showcase your personality and connect with someone on a more human level. They can feel your energy and presence, and you can connect with them more vulnerably and uniquely. I have met people in person who, if they had met me online, would probably have had a different understanding of my personal journey. With in-person networking, you can bounce off each other and build up a rapport like no other.'

Online platforms offer a valuable space for initial engagement – following admired individuals, commenting on posts, and showing support – and help forge connections that might not be possible otherwise due to geographical or temporal constraints. But offline networking allows connection and rapport-building that is difficult to replicate digitally. The physical presence, energy and potential for vulnerability in face-to-face meetings enhances the authenticity of the interaction, providing opportunities for individuals to connect on a more human level. This direct engagement enables people to showcase their personalities more fully and understand each other's journeys better.

The challenge of balancing online and offline community engagement lies in leveraging the strengths of each approach. While online engagement can facilitate connections and support, the essence of networking lies in the personal, in-depth interactions that occur offline. In-person meetings allow a more complete exchange of ideas and experiences, reinforcing the concept that 'people buy into people'.

James McGough also shared some insight on how he balances online and offline engagement, and what key ingredients he thinks online engagement misses. James is a managing director at Clarion Events, one of the world's leading event organizers who supports communities in every major sector across Europe, Asia, Africa and America. He is passionate about developing people, teams and businesses internationally, and sits on executive boards for the Association of Event Organisers and Women in Exhibitions.

'During lockdown,' he shared, 'we couldn't run in-person events, and the impact on individuals, businesses and communities was more seismic than we could have ever imagined. It impacted career growth, business sales and the speed of innovation across many industries. In my experience, online networking misses three key ingredients.'

SERENDIPITY

Serendipity is when events occur and develop by chance in a happy or beneficial way.

'There is no real substitute for in-person networking when it comes to meeting people who have similar interests, challenges and opportunities as you,' said James. 'Particularly if you are looking to meet more senior influential figureheads who are generally quite absent or dismissive of online platforms. In-person events provide "sliding doors" moments. Often you can bump into someone at an event while getting a coffee or grabbing lunch and these end up being the most valuable connections. Each day, busy people get 100+ emails, 20+ cold calls and 10+ LinkedIn connections. Cutting through the noise online is just hard. And, we have the evidence to back this up. When we had to run virtual instead of in-person events during COVID, attendee satisfaction for networking and the number of connections made plummeted.'

AUTHENTICITY

Authenticity is the quality of being real or true.

'The most effective human interaction requires us to be able to use all of our senses,' James told me. 'To look beyond a screen or an avatar. Meeting someone in person helps to build trust and to build relationships faster. Eye contact, body language and the way that we connect with someone can't be replaced by video conferencing or chat rooms. It takes more effort to meet someone in person, which is often more appreciated as it shows that we are serious and that we care.'

EFFICIENCY

Efficiency is the ability to produce results in the quickest time without wasting effort.

'It's possible to achieve more during a five-minute in-person interaction than you could in five hours of Zoom calls,' said James. 'Your ability to create an impression, to make an impact and to be remembered is exponentially higher than an online interaction. In a world where people are bombarded by online messages, notifications, chats and relentless Zoom calls, it's hard to stand out from the crowd. If you want to make an impression on an individual or a community, my advice would be to "show up". In person.'

These three critical elements – serendipity, authenticity and efficiency – are often diminished or entirely absent in digital networking contexts, but they each have a huge impact on personal and professional development.

Here are some of the ways you can ensure you keep a balance. Addressing these aspects is key to building a sustainable community in our increasingly digital world.

I. DEEPENING CONNECTIONS BEYOND THE SCREEN

Online platforms offer remarkable tools for initial engagement, allowing people from various backgrounds to connect

COMMUNITY IN A DIGITAL AGE

irrespective of geography or physical access. However, the depth and authenticity of face-to-face interactions is unparalleled. Be intentional about connecting beyond the screen and where possible prioritize in-person meetings.

2. ENSURING INCLUSIVITY AND ACCESSIBILITY

The digital divide remains a persistent issue, with certain segments of the population lacking either the skills or the means to engage effectively online. Community leaders can craft engagement strategies that are not only digitally inclusive but also accessible to those less inclined or able to participate online.

3. COMBATING DIGITAL FATIGUE AND PROMOTING WELL-BEING

With the surge in digital communication, especially post-pandemic, digital fatigue has become increasingly common. You should provide community members with offline engagement opportunities that offer a digital detox and enhance well-being.

4. BUILDING TRUST THROUGH PERSONAL INTERACTIONS

The establishment of trust and authenticity is often more effective in person. Body language, tone of voice and immediate feedback all play a crucial role in building genuine relationships.

Reflect with Raphael

- *How can communities harness online tools to initiate and develop connections that eventually translate into real-world relationships?*
- *In what ways can community activities be structured to incorporate both online and offline elements, thereby enriching the overall community experience?*
- *What strategies can be implemented to provide community members with offline engagement opportunities that offer a digital detox and enhance well-being?*
- *How can this online and offline integration be achieved seamlessly, and what creative approaches can be utilized to ensure that both digital and physical spaces are contributing effectively to the community's growth and cohesion?*

CHAPTER 10

Sustaining a Thriving Community for Long-Term Success

The challenge often lies not just in the creation of community but in sustaining it for long-term success.

Community is measured not only by an initial groundswell of enthusiasm but by its ability to evolve, adapt and thrive over time. Research reveals that communities with sustained engagement and active participation exhibit higher success rates when it comes to achieving their long-term goals – highlighting the crucial role of sustainability in community success.[70]

As the Greek philosopher Heraclitus famously said, 'Change is the only constant in life.' Sustaining a thriving community requires a delicate balance of maintaining its core values while adapting to changing circumstances.

The sustainability of a community hinges on the strength of the relationships and the sense of belonging among its members. The *Harvard Business Review* emphasizes that communities with strong interpersonal connections report higher levels of member satisfaction and, crucially, retention.[71]

The long-term success of a community also depends on its ability to generate value for its members. This value can come in various forms – support, knowledge, networking opportunities or a sense of purpose. As management expert Peter Drucker once observed, 'The most important thing in communication is hearing what isn't said.'

In the context of community-building, leaders must be attuned to the unspoken needs and aspirations of their members in order to deliver value continuously for them – something that Jamelia Donaldson emphasized when we spoke. 'The quiet voices within a community often hold the true gems of wisdom and inspiration. By attuning to unspoken needs, you can observe patterns, note subtle cues, and be empathetic to the emotions conveyed through non-verbal communication. Facilitating opportunities for anonymous feedback ensures that even those who prefer to remain in the background feel heard and valued.'

Jamelia's insight highlights the reality that not all community members are vocal about their thoughts, concerns and ideas, yet their contributions can be invaluable. Accessing these requires a leader to be observant, empathetic, and proactive in creating inclusive feedback mechanisms.

Resilience is also a key part of sustaining a community. Izzy Obeng shared some of the key factors that she believes make a community strong and resilient: 'A strong community, for me, thrives on a shared vision for the future and a fervent, collective energy towards a common goal. Resilience comes from a shared history that brings pride and a deep reserve of collective memory that a community can draw from. Together, that strength and that resilience can fuel adaptation, innovation and persistence in the face of challenges.

'As a Black British woman, I know that I stand on the shoulders of giants. In just my lifetime I can name incredible leaders like Dr Yvonne Thompson CBE, Baroness Lawrence of Clarendon, Dr Anne-Marie Imafidon MBE and Dame Vivian Hunt, who have paved the way in their respective industries and inspired the generation after them.

'We started Foundervine with one clear vision – to build a world with no social or economic barriers to innovation. That vision has driven us far beyond where we thought we would be, and has led us into the very seats of power in the UK, whether that has been Number 10 Downing Street with the prime minister's business team or to Buckingham Palace for an audience with the Duke and Duchess of Sussex.

'We do what we do, helping founders from underserved communities build businesses because a community is only as strong as its leaders, its innovators, its creators. These are the people that have the audacity to believe that they can change their communities for the better – that they can change the world. A community comes around these people, pushing them, encouraging them and recognizing that if they win, the rest of the community wins as well.'

Resilience is deeply rooted in a community's shared history and pride. Izzy's reference to standing on the 'shoulders of giants' reflects the importance of role models and trailblazers in shaping a community's identity and aspirations. These individuals, driven by a belief in their capacity to effect positive change, embody the essence of community strength. The community's support for these changemakers, through encouragement and recognition, shows the symbiotic relationship between individual aspirations and collective well-being.

Sustaining a thriving community is an ongoing process that requires foresight, adaptability, and a deep understanding of the human aspects of community dynamics. The challenge for leaders is to keep their community engaged and relevant, ensuring its longevity and success.

Reflect with Raphael

- *How can you ensure that your community remains relevant and adaptive in the face of inevitable changes, whether they be in interests, goals or external environments?*
- *How can you cultivate and nurture relationships to develop a sense of commitment among community members?*
- *How can you attune yourself to the unspoken needs and aspirations of your members to continuously deliver value?*

Here are some of the key ways you can build a community with lasting impact and relevance.

1. ESTABLISH AND CONSTANTLY COMMUNICATE A TRANSPARENT VISION

James McGough told me the following: 'For me, transparency is one of the key values for my teams. Each year we have four "business update" meetings, kicking off in January, where we share strategic objectives, budgets and stretch targets. We check in on progress and report back to the whole team on a weekly and quarterly basis to make sure everyone remains connected to the direction of travel. Everyone can contribute ideas and there is no such thing as a stupid question.

'During these meetings and throughout the year I trust them with information that other leaders might feel uncomfortable with . . . Why? Because trust is reciprocated. It leads to people feeling empowered and feeling that they have a clear purpose with their roles and responsibilities and that they contribute towards results.

'Providing that we as leaders have the right level of resources, systems and processes, having a clear and transparent strategy leads to a far more motivated group. Having a plan of how to get from A to B also reduces stress and anxiety so we can all enjoy the journey far more!

'One of the most effective management tools that we use for team alignment and productivity with delivering our strategy is the "RACI". This outlines who is Responsible, Accountable, Consulted and Informed across the many projects and tasks that we have to complete. Every individual in the team is assigned a role in delivering our strategy, which creates a collective energy and drive.

'We also map the RACI to each individual's personal development plan. So, if for example someone was consulted or informed about a project this year, we may look to give them more responsibility or final accountability next year. This visualizes progression for individuals, which again can be motivating and helps to align everyone around a longer-term strategic plan.'

2. PARTICIPATION AND OWNERSHIP

A community thrives when its members feel a sense of ownership and are involved in its activities. Creating opportunities for members to contribute, lead initiatives, and have a voice in decision-making is crucial to community longevity.

3. ADAPT AND EVOLVE

A community's ability to remain relevant depends on its adaptability to changing member needs and external environments. This involves continuously gathering feedback, staying attuned to trends and being willing to innovate. Chris Skeith believes that the 'key to evolution and adaptation is to listen intently to the voices that surround you. From customers and teams to fans and detractors, each perspective contributes to the mosaic of understanding and hints towards how you can adapt. The key is not just to hear but to truly listen, extracting insights that may be hidden on first hearing.'

4. SUSTAINABLE GROWTH STRATEGIES

Sustainable growth involves balancing the expansion of the community with the maintenance of its core values and quality of interactions. Communities that focus on sustainable growth involving strategic planning and careful resource allocation are more likely to retain long-term engagement.

Chris Skeith shared some of the key factors that helped him sustain his community, and discussed its beginnings. 'I joined the world of association management and the trade and consumer show sector to unite two associations, one long-established and the other a newer entity. As I stepped into this realm, both boards had already committed to a merger, contingent upon resolving a comprehensive seventeen-point plan within the span of a year.

'Each association brought its unique positives, protagonists and personalities to the table. The vision was clear: by joining forces, they could become a more robust and representative force within their community. The linchpin for success lay in ensuring that both entities felt equally valued, heard, and vested in the evolution of any new solutions.

'Over the ensuing twelve months, meticulous attention was dedicated to addressing each point of the plan. Every board member was consulted regularly, and bi-monthly board meetings provided a collective platform to track progress. Open dialogue, transparency and honesty became the cornerstones of our approach.

'Encountering occasional heated discussions, the commitment to resolving issues through investigation and identification of options and solutions never wavered. With diligence and hard work, consensus was achieved on all seventeen points, and the associations successfully merged within the year.

'In the transition to the new organization, a remarkable outcome emerged – not a single member departed.

On the contrary, a more robust and united community took shape, focused on common issues, wielding a stronger voice, and exerting a more substantial influence in the industry. The journey was a testament to the power of collaboration, open communication and shared commitment, illustrating that with hard work, honesty and good communication the seemingly impossible merger was indeed possible.'

This successful unification of a long-established association and a newer entity formed by dissenters showcases several key strategies for ensuring long-term success in community-building efforts.

First, the importance of a clear, shared vision. The mutual agreement on becoming a more robust and representative force within their industry provided a common goal that guided the merger process. This shared vision acted as a unifying force, helping to bridge differences and motivate both parties towards a collective outcome.

Second, ensuring equal value, voice and investment in the evolution of the new entity. This crucial strategy allowed inclusivity and equity in community integration, ensuring that all members felt their contributions and concerns were respected and addressed. By prioritizing open dialogue, transparency and honesty, the merger process created a culture of trust and collaboration, which is essential for sustainable community growth.

Third, regular consultations and bi-monthly board meetings facilitated a structured yet flexible framework for tracking progress and maintaining open lines of communication. This consistent engagement helped to pre-empt potential conflicts and ensured that all stakeholders were aligned with the merger's progress and objectives.

The successful resolution of a comprehensive seventeen-point plan, achieved through diligent investigation, discussion and consensus-building, highlights the effectiveness of such a methodical and inclusive approach to conflict resolution and strategic planning. The fact that no members departed during the transition to the new organization is a remarkable testament to the success of these strategies, as there was a strong sense of community loyalty and buy-in to the new direction.

Ultimately, Chris's example illustrates that sustainable growth and long-term success in community management are achievable through a combination of shared vision, inclusivity, open communication and diligent planning and execution.

Reflect with Raphael

- *How do you create a community that not only stands the test of time but also evolves and is a meaningful space for your members?*
- *How can community leaders craft and communicate a vision that inspires and aligns with the core values of its members?*
- *How can leaders encourage active participation create avenues for members to take on leadership roles?*

Measuring Success and Continuously Improving Your Community

Measuring success and continuous improvement involves a sophisticated blend of objective analysis and subjective understanding. It's about setting up systems that not only track progress but align with the community's core values and aspirations.

For Cecil Peters, the two most significant key metrics for measuring success are 'a sense of inclusion, and safety'. He explained: 'If you feel that your opinion is welcome and valued, if you feel that your complaints will be listened to and investigated fairly, if you feel that you won't suffer repercussions for expressing your dissatisfaction, then that is a good environment.'

These elements are foundational to creating an environment where members feel valued, respected and secure, all of which are critical for sustaining a thriving community over the long term. Ensuring that members' opinions are welcome, complaints are fairly investigated, and dissatisfaction can be expressed without fear of repercussions demonstrates a commitment to transparency, accountability and open communication. These principles are essential for building trust and engagement among community members.

Measuring success requires a nuanced understanding of community dynamics and a proactive approach to addressing issues that may arise. For a community to thrive and sustain long-term success, it is crucial to continuously monitor and improve inclusivity and safety. This means not only reacting to feedback and incidents as they occur, but also actively seeking out opportunities to enhance these aspects in the long term.

Continuous improvement is complex, requiring a culture that values learning and adapts to feedback, and that embraces a mindset where trial and error are seen as integral to growth, and every failure is dissected to learn valuable lessons.

Here are some of the key strategies you can use to measure success and continuously improve your community.

1. DEVELOP COMPREHENSIVE METRICS

Beyond basic numbers like membership count or event attendance, it's important to establish a broad set of metrics that reflects the community's health and vibrancy. These might include member engagement levels, satisfaction surveys and the impact of community initiatives. Using tools like the Net Promoter Score (NPS) can gauge member loyalty and overall satisfaction.

2. CULTIVATE A FEEDBACK-RICH ENVIRONMENT

Encourage and facilitate ongoing feedback from community members. This could be through regular surveys, suggestion boxes or open forums. Feedback should be seen as a valuable resource for improvement.

3. IMPLEMENT REGULAR REVIEW AND ADAPTATION CYCLES

Schedule periodic reviews of community activities and strategies based on the established metrics and feedback. Use these reviews to identify areas for improvement and adapt or develop new strategies in response.

4. CREATE A CULTURE OF CONTINUOUS LEARNING AND INNOVATION

Encourage a mindset of learning and innovation within the community. This involves being open to new ideas, willing to experiment, and learning from both successes and failures.

Reflect with Raphael

- *How can you create an environment where risk-taking is encouraged, and every setback is viewed as a stepping stone to greater understanding and adaptability?*
- *How can you effectively communicate the ongoing process of evaluation and improvement, making it an inclusive and collective journey?*
- *What specific metrics best align with your community's goals, and how regularly should they be evaluated for a true reflection of the community's health?*
- *What initiatives can you introduce to develop a culture of continuous learning and innovation among your community members?*

Words of Wisdom

I asked some of my contributors and other community leaders what community meant to them, and they came up with the following words of wisdom.

Asif Mohammed

'Community is where one feels a part of something. Some feel this through their work, or being part of a sports group, religious society or arts and culture group.'

Rebekah Taitt

'A place where I share a common interest or sense of belonging or goal as others, due to similar characteristics or attitudes. The right community brings enrichment to life itself.'

Andy Ayim

'As I've grown older and travelled the world, you realize that community isn't limited by boundaries and lines as there is more that we have in common as humanity than what separates us.'

Annisha Taylor

'Interpersonal connections offer opportunities for self-reflection, feedback and growth. Through interactions with others, we gain insights into our own thoughts, feelings and behaviours.'

Cecil Peters

'Community, to me, is being in a space where I am encouraged to be the best version of myself I can be, and where help is offered when it is needed.'

Chris Skeith

'Community is everything, communities are unique; their ability to drive change, support individuals, groups and causes is invaluable. When you find one that matches your values and personality, embrace it and go all in.

'Communities are vibrant with changing needs, and engaging to help adapt to those changes is exciting, challenging and hugely rewarding. Everyone has the power to make a difference, start engaging today!'

Elizabeth Uviebinené

'Community means home, a place where I am welcomed and supported.'

Indie Gordon

'In the dynamic landscape of our ever-changing world, community stands as the bold catalyst for innovation. Here, iron sharpens iron, a testament to shared strength that fuels growth, forges connections, and becomes an essential force for navigating the challenges of our evolving landscape. Together, we transform individual sparks into a blazing trail of collective brilliance, forging a path towards a brighter, interconnected future.'

Jamelia Donaldson

'Community, stemming from the word "communication", is a sanctuary and network of interconnected individuals. It serves as a safe space with the primary intention of facilitating information exchange, rallying behind shared causes, concerns or experiences, and engaging in reciprocal learning.'

Kanya King

'Community, to me, means people coming together to support each other, collaborate rather than compete, and create a supportive ecosystem where everyone can thrive. It's about contributing to the well-being of family, friends, the wider community and the country.'

Karen Wardle

'Community for me means the bringing together of people who share the same purpose. Whether that be personally or professionally, for a community to be effective its members need to align to its purpose and then continually bring their experience, passion and knowledge to the community to help it grow and succeed.'

Leroy A. Bryan

'Community is a gathering space where individuals converge to exchange ideas and perspectives, which fosters a profound sense of unity. This communal spirit has been instrumental in the growth of my business, primarily through word-of-mouth endorsements. In particular my business provides a space for men where they can open up and talk about their feelings. Indeed, community is both the cornerstone of and foundation upon which my business thrives.'

Lynsey Campbell

'Community to me is all about sharing purpose and values with others, working alongside a group of others who bring out the best in you and amplify and celebrate your strengths.'

Mac Alonge

'Real community consists of the people that fill your life with the unseen things that you need to thrive – joy, support, guidance, collaboration and inspiration. Community lifts you up when you are down or at risk of falling down, and celebrates/champions you when you're flying high.'

Margaret Boatemaah

'Communities are support systems, offering spaces where relationships can be formed and individuals grow.'

Melina Mavoungou

'When I think of community, I think of the people that I want to share the good, bad and ugly with. Those that cry when I cry and rejoice when I have things to celebrate. Those that challenge me when I'm wrong and encourage me to push past my comfort zone. Friendships that are high-quality but relatively low-maintenance, with an understanding that everyone has their own lives, families, goals and ambitions.'

Mike Sealy

'My quote on how I view a community is "it takes a village". It is such a powerful quote, one that is not always well understood until you really take time to reflect and understand what it means on a personal level. It comes from the proverb 'it takes a village to raise a child', which describes how a community comes together to raise a child, i.e. parents, teachers, extended family, neighbours look out for the safety, protection, guidance and education of a child. This is how I view communities, who come together, support each other, share knowledge and best practice, give advice when needed, etc.'

Opeyemi Sofoluke

'Community is all about connection – a physical and, in some cases, a spiritual space where we can relate to others and forge bonds through shared experiences. It is a space we should never take for granted, as its true value often becomes apparent only in its absence. Personally, my communities have been a blessing, reminding me that, regardless of the journey, I'm not alone. Within these circles of connection, I've encountered individuals who encourage, support and uplift me. I've also appreciated those who challenge and push me in ways I never knew I needed. My advice to anyone within a community is to cherish genuine connections, recognizing that each of us has something valuable to contribute.'

Remel London

'Community is knowing that a group of like-minded individuals can rally together to support, raise awareness, protect or celebrate a collective cause or for an occasion that they are all passionate about.'

Scarlett Allen-Horton

'All for one and one for all (without sounding like the Three Musketeers!) – we are all in this together, with each other and for each other.'

Shelley Bishton

'Community is an anchor of allegiance. It provides a sense of shared purpose and values, and overarching support.'

Stefan Johnson

'True community is where collective individuals can be their authentic self, cultivated by positive values and unburdened by pretence.'

Tayo Oguntonade

'A community is where our voices find listeners. We hold a profound belief in the power of impact and purpose, and we recognize that each individual holds a vital responsibility to contribute positively to their community.'

Acknowledgements

A huge thank you to Cameron Myers and Oscar-Janson Smith for having faith in me to deliver this important book about what makes our communities tick. A big thank you goes out to everyone at Penguin Business for being there for me on this adventure.

To my family, friends, and everyone else who's been part of this journey: your support means the world to me. I appreciate you always being there to cheer me on and for giving me that push whenever I start to doubt myself. I couldn't have come this far without you all by my side.

As iron sharpens iron, so one person sharpens another.

Proverbs 27:17

Notes

1. 'History of Blue Zones', Blue Zones, https://www.bluezones.com/about/history/.
2. Marguerite Deslauriers and Zoli Filotas, 'Aristotle's Human Beings', in Karolina Hübner (ed.), *Human*, Oxford University Press, 2022, https://doi.org/10.1093/oso/9780190876371.003.0003.
3. Ryan Erskine, '22 Statistics That Prove the Value of Personal Branding', Entrepreneur, 13 September 2016, https://www.entrepreneur.com/starting-a-business/22-statistics-that-prove-the-value-of-personal-branding/280371.
4. Emma Brudner, 'The Ultimate Guide to Personal Branding', HubSpot, 12 May 2022, https://blog.hubspot.com/sales/the-ultimate-guide-to-personal-branding.
5. https://dictionary.cambridge.org/dictionary/english/leverage.
6. Victoria Novik, 'Cultural Sensitivity in Design: Why It Matters and How to Develop It', Medium, 28 June 2023, https://victorianovik.medium.com/cultural-sensitivity-in-design-why-it-matters-and-how-to-develop-it-6f27b590bec5.
7. Deborah Weinswig, 'Influencers Are the New Brands', *Forbes*, 5 October 2019, https://www.forbes.com/sites/deborahweinswig/2016/10/05/influencers-are-the-new-brands.
8. Serenity Gibbons, 'You And Your Business Have 7 Seconds To Make A First Impression: Here's How To Succeed', *Forbes*, 19 June 2018, www.forbes.com/sites/serenitygibbons/2018/06/19/you-have-7-seconds-to-make-a-first-impression-heres-how-to-succeed.

9. https://vwo.com/ab-testing.
10. Ekaterina Walter, '50 Heavyweight Leadership Quotes', *Forbes*, 30 September 2013, https://www.forbes.com/sites/ekaterinawal ter/2013/09/30/50-heavyweight-leadership-quotes/.
11. '8 Employee Engagement Statistics You Need to Know', HR Cloud, 9 June 2022, https://www.hrcloud.com/blog/ 8-employee-engagement-statistics-you-need-to-know.
12. Christina Folz, 'Lazslo Bock's Tips for Building a Better Workplace', SHRM, https://www.shrm.org/topics-tools/ news/laszlo-bocks-6-tips-building-better-workplace.
13. '3 Ways to Build Trust as a Leader', Crestcom, 20 May 2021, https:// crestcom.com/blog/2021/05/20/3-ways-build-trust-leader/.
14. 'How diversity helps companies to succeed', McKinsey & Company, February 2020, https://www.mckinsey.com/~/ media/McKinsey/Email/Classics/2020/2020-02-classic.html.
15. Janet H. Cho, 'Diversity is being invited to the party', Cleveland.com, 25 May 2016, https://www.cleveland.com/ business/2016/05/diversity_is_being_invited_to.html.
16. Rocio Lorenzo and Martin Reeves, 'How and Where Diversity Drives Financial Performance', *Harvard Business Review*, 30 January 2018, https://hbr.org/2018/01/how-and-where- diversity-drives-financial-performance.
17. Herminia Ibarra and Mark Lee Hunter, 'How Leaders Create and Use Networks', *Harvard Business Review*, January 2007, https://hbr.org/2007/01/how-leaders-create-and-use-networks.
18. 'Important Networking Statistics Everyone Should Know', Apollo Technical, 17 January 2023, https://www.apollotechnical. com/networking-statistics/.
19. David W. McMillan and David Chavis, 'Sense of Community: A Definition and Theory', *Journal of Community and Psychology*, 14(1), January 1986, pp. 6–23, https://www.researchgate.net/ publication/235356904_Sense_of_Community_A_Definition_ and_Theory.

20. Saul McLeod, 'Maslow's Hierarchy of Needs', Simply Psychology, 24 January 2024, https://www.simplypsychology.org/maslow.html.

21. Suzanne de Janasz and Maury Pieperl, 'CEOs Need Mentors Too', *Harvard Business Review*, April 2015, https://hbr.org/2015/04/ceos-need-mentors-too.

22. Mind, *Introduction to Mentally Healthy Workplaces*, https://www.mind.org.uk/media-a/4663/resource1_mentally_healthy_workplacesfinal_pdf.pdf.

23. 'Helping Employees Deal with Change in the Workplace', Bravo, 12 March 2019, https://www.bravowell.com/resources/helping-employees-deal-with-change-in-the-workplace.

24. 'Carl Gustav Jung', Oxford Reference, https://www.oxfordreference.com/display/10.1093/acref/9780191826719.001.0001/q-oro-ed4-00006107.

25. 'Stress in America 2020', American Psychological Association, October 2020, https://www.apa.org/news/press/releases/stress/2020/report-october.

26. Ali Rogin and Claire Mufson, 'Researchers Find Strong Relationships Protect Long-Term Health and Happiness', *PBS News*, 26 November 2023, https://www.pbs.org/newshour/show/researchers-find-strong-relationships-protect-long-term-health-and-happiness.

27. 'Susan Pinker: What Makes Social Connection So Vital to Our Well-Being?', TED Radio Hour, 24 April 2020, https://www.npr.org/transcripts/842604367.

28. Public Health Service, *Our Epidemic of Loneliness and Isolation*, 2023, https://www.hhs.gov/sites/default/files/surgeon-general-social-connection-advisory.pdf.

29. https://ohio4h.org/sites/ohio4h/files/imce/Emotional%20Intelligence%20Background.pdf.

30. B. X. Ngooi et al., 'Exploring the use of activity-based group therapy in increasing self-efficacy and subjective well-being in acute mental health', *Hong Kong Journal of Occupational*

Therapy, 35(1), June 2022, pp. 52–61, https://doi.org/ 10.1177/ 15691861221075798.

31. David S. Lee et al., '1-Through-We', *Personality and Social Psychology Bulletin*, 44(1), 2018, pp. 37–48, https://websites. umich.edu/~gonzo/papers/lee-2017-i-we.pdf.

32. 'The nature of loneliness', *University of Chicago Magazine*, https://magazine.uchicago.edu/1012/features/the-nature-of-loneliness.shtml.

33. 'Volunteer Impacts', NCVO, https://www.ncvo.org.uk/news-and-insights/news-index/time-well-spent-national-survey-volunteer-experience/volunteer-impacts/.

34. 'Why Do Friendships Matter?', *House Calls* podcast, 24 January 2023, https://www.hhs.gov/surgeongeneral/priorities/house-calls/dr-marisa-g-franco-part-1/index.html.

35. 'How to make friends?', KU News, 6 March 2018, https://news. ku.edu/2018/03/06/study-reveals-number-hours-it-takes-make-friend.

36. *Diversity Wins: How Inclusion Matters*, McKinsey & Company, 19 May 2020, https://www.mckinsey.com/featured-insights/ diversity-and-inclusion/diversity-wins-how-inclusion-matters.

37. Alison Reynolds and David Lewis, 'Teams Solve Problems Faster When They're More Cognitively Diverse, *Harvard Business Review*, 30 March 2017, https://hbr.org/2017/03/teams-solve-problems-faster-when-theyre-more-cognitively-diverse.

38. S. A. Hewlett et al., 'Diversity's Positive Impact on Innovation and Outcomes', *The Global Talent Competitiveness Index 2018*, https://www.talentinnovation.org/ Diversity%C3%A2%E2%82%AC%E2%84%A2s-Positive-Impact-on-Innovation-and-Outcomes-CTI-Chapter.pdf.

39. Erik Larson, infographic, https://www.cloverpop.com/blog/ infographic-diversity-inclusion-better-decision-making-at-work.

40. Mary Kite and Patricia Clark, 'The benefits of diversity education', American Psychological Association, 8 September

2022, https://www.apa.org/ed/precollege/psychology-teacher-network/introductory-psychology/benefits-of-diversity.

41. Deloitte, *The Economic Benefits of Improving Social Inclusion*, August 2019, https://www2.deloitte.com/content/dam/Deloitte/my/Documents/risk/my-risk-sdg10-economic-benefits-of-improving-social-inclusion.pdf.

42. National League of Cities, *Bright Spots in Community Engagement*, https://knightfoundation.org/wp-content/uploads/2019/06/BrightSpots-final.pdf.

43. Juliet Bourke, 'The diversity and inclusion revolution: Eight powerful truths', *Deloitte Review*, 22, https://www2.deloitte.com/us/en/insights/deloitte-review/issue-22/diversity-and-inclusion-at-work-eight-powerful-truths.html.

44. M. Alegría et al., 'Social Determinants of Mental Health: Where We Are and Where We Need to Go', *Curr Psychiatry Rep*, 20(11), September 2018, p. 95, https://doi.org/10.1007/s11920-018-0969-9.

45. Evan Carr et al., 'The Value of Belonging at Work', *Harvard Business Review*, 16 December 2019, https://hbr.org/2019/12/the-value-of-belonging-at-work.

46. Gifford Thomas, 'Leadership is not about being in charge', Leadership First, 7 July 2022, https://www.leadershipfirst.net/post/leadership-is-not-about-being-in-charge.

47. Bill Gentry, 'The Importance of Empathy in the Workplace', Center for Creative Leadership, 28 January 2023, https://www.ccl.org/articles/leading-effectively-articles/empathy-in-the-workplace-a-tool-for-effective-leadership/.

48. 'Why inclusive leadership is so vital to D&I', ICAEW, 15 February 2022, https://www.icaew.com/insights/diversity-and-inclusion/welcome-inclusion/why-inclusive-leadership-is-so-vital-to-di.

49. Ilya Pozin, '16 Leadership Quotes', *Forbes*, 10 April 2014, https://www.forbes.com/sites/ilyapozin/2014/04/10/16-leadership-quotes-to-inspire-you-to-greatness/.

50. D. J. Kleynhans et al., 'Authentic Leadership, Trust (in the Leader), and Flourishing: Does Precariousness Matter?', *Frontiers in Psychology*, 13, April 2022, 798759, https://doi.org/10.3389/fpsyg.2022.798759.

51. N. Jankelová and Z. Joniaková, 'Communication Skills and Transformational Leadership Style of First-Line Nurse Managers in Relation to Job Satisfaction of Nurses and Moderators of This Relationship', *Healthcare* (Basel), 9(3), March 2020, p. 346, https://doi.org/10.3390/healthcare9030346.

52. Conor Kenny, 'The single biggest problem in communication is the illusion that it has taken place', *Irish Times*, 9 November 2020, https://www.irishtimes.com/culture/books/the-single-biggest-problem-in-communication-is-the-illusion-that-it-has-taken-place-1.4404586.

53. Lauren Landry, 'Why emotional intelligence is important in leadership', Harvard Business School Online, 3 April 2019, https://online.hbs.edu/blog/post/emotional-intelligence-in-leadership.

54. Daniel Goleman, 'Working with Emotional Intelligence', *New York Times*, 1998, https://archive.nytimes.com/www.nytimes.com/books/first/g/goleman-working.html.

55. Hannes Leroy et al., 'Walking our Evidence-Based Walk', *Journal of Leadership and Organizational Studies*, 29(1), January 2022, https://journals.sagepub.com/doi/10.1177/15480518211062563.

56. H. Khan et al., 'Impact of transformational leadership on work performance, burnout and social loafing: a mediation model', *Future Business Journal*, 6(40), 2020, https://doi.org/10.1186/s43093-020-00043-8.

57. 'Leading with Compassion Has Research-Backed Benefits', *Harvard Business Review*, 27 February 2023, https://hbr.org/2023/02/leading-with-compassion-has-research-backed-benefits.

58. *McKinsey Global Surveys 2021, A Year In Review*, https://www.mckinsey.com/~/media/mckinsey/featured%20insights/

mckinsey%20global%20surveys/mckinsey-global-surveys-2021-a-year-in-review.pdf.

59. Marcia Blenko et al., 'The Decision-Driven Organization', *Harvard Business Review*, June 2010, https://hbr.org/2010/06/the-decision-driven-organization.

60. 'Adapting to Change Requires Flexible Leaders', Center for Creative Leadership, 24 August 2021, https://www.ccl.org/articles/leading-effectively-articles/adaptability-1-idea-3-facts-5-tips/.

61. See https://www.youtube.com/watch?v=UedER6ioUy4.

62. Michael Gilmartin and Emily Hogan, 'Enhancing workforce resilience through recognition', Insights2Action, 30 May 2023, https://action.deloitte.com/insight/3367/enhancing-workforce-resilience-through-recognition.

63. Dave Chaffey, 'Global social media statistics 2024', https://www.smartinsights.com/social-media-marketing/social-media-strategy/new-global-social-media-research/.

64. 'Americans' views of and experiences with activism on social media', Pew Research Center, 29 June 2023, https://www.pewresearch.org/internet/2023/06/29/americans-views-of-and-experiences-with-activism-on-social-media/.

65. Rebecca Riserbato, '10 benefits of consistent, high-quality marketing', HubSpot, 27 October 2021, https://blog.hubspot.com/marketing/benefits-high-quality-content-consistency-brand.

66. https://business.adobe.com/blog/basics/digital-marketing-campaign-examples.

67. Adam Connell, '28 Latest Social Media Statistics For 2024: What Is The State Of Social Media?', 20 March 2024, https://bloggingwizard.com/social-media-statistics-facts-trends/.

68. 'Nonverbal Communication: How Body Language & Nonverbal Cues Are Key', Lifesize, 18 February 2020, https://www.lifesize.com/blog/speaking-without-words.

69. H. Beyari, 'The Relationship between Social Media and the Increase in Mental Health Problems', *International Journal of Environmental Research and Public Health*, 20(3), January 2023, 2383, https:doi.org/10.3390/ijerph2003238.
70. CPID, *Learning and Skills at Work: Survey 2021*, https://www.cipd.org/globalassets/media/comms/news/as2learning-skills-work-report-2021-1_tcm18-95433.pdf.
71. Matthew Dixon et al., 'Stop Trying to Delight Your Customers', *Harvard Business Review*, July–August 2010, https://hbr.org/2010/07/stop-trying-to-delight-your-customers.